SEPTEMBER 2023

S	M	T	W	T	F	S
					1 15 ELUL	**2** 16 ELUL Parashat Ki Tavo
3 17 ELUL	**4** 18 ELUL Labor Day (US & Canada)	**5** 19 ELUL	**6** 20 ELUL	**7** 21 ELUL	**8** 22 ELUL	**9** 23 ELUL Selihot Parashat Nitzavim-Vayelech
10 24 ELUL	**11** 25 ELUL	**12** 26 ELUL	**13** 27 ELUL	**14** 28 ELUL	**15** 29 ELUL Rosh Hashanah (Begins at Sundown) Erev Rosh Ha-Shanah	**16** 1 TISHRI Rosh Ha-Shanah 5784
17 2 TISHRI Rosh Ha-Shanah	**18** 3 TISHRI Fast of Gedaliah	**19** 4 TISHRI	**20** 5 TISHRI	**21** 6 TISHRI International Day of Peace	**22** 7 TISHRI	**23** 8 TISHRI First Day of Autumn Shabbat Shuva Parashat Ha'Azinu
24 9 TISHRI Yom Kippur (Begins at Sundown) Erev Yom Kippur	**25** 10 TISHRI Yom Kippur Yizkor	**26** 11 TISHRI	**27** 12 TISHRI	**28** 13 TISHRI	**29** 14 TISHRI Full Moon Erev Sukkot	**30** 15 TISHRI National Day for Truth and Reconciliation (Canada) First Day of Sukkot

27 Sunday		10

NOTES

28 Monday		11

Summer Bank Holiday (UK)

29 Tuesday		12

30 Wednesday		13

Full Moon

31 Thursday		14

1 Friday		15

August 2023

S	M	T	W	T	F	S
		1	2	3	4	5
6	7	8	9	10	11	12
13	14	15	16	17	18	19
20	21	22	23	24	25	26
27	28	29	30	31		

2 Saturday	Parashat Ki Tavo	16

September 2023

S	M	T	W	T	F	S
					1	2
3	4	5	6	7	8	9
10	11	12	13	14	15	16
17	18	19	20	21	22	23
24	25	26	27	28	29	30

SEPTEMBER 2023

NOTES

_____
_____
_____
_____
_____
_____
_____
_____
_____
_____
_____
_____
_____
_____
_____
_____
_____
_____
_____
_____

3 Sunday | 17

4 Monday | 18

Labor Day (US & Canada)

5 Tuesday | 19

6 Wednesday | 20

7 Thursday | 21

8 Friday | 22

September 2023

S	M	T	W	T	F	S
					1	2
3	4	5	6	7	8	9
10	11	12	13	14	15	16
17	18	19	20	21	22	23
24	25	26	27	28	29	30

October 2023

S	M	T	W	T	F	S
1	2	3	4	5	6	7
8	9	10	11	12	13	14
15	16	17	18	19	20	21
22	23	24	25	26	27	28
29	30	31				

9 Saturday | Selihot | 23
Parashat Nitzavim-Vayelech

SEPTEMBER 2023

10	Sunday		24

11	Monday		25

12	Tuesday		26

13	Wednesday		27

14	Thursday		28

15	Friday	Erev Rosh Ha-Shanah	29

Rosh Hashanah (Begins at Sundown)

16	Saturday	Rosh Ha-Shanah 5784	1

NOTES

September 2023

S	M	T	W	T	F	S
					1	2
3	4	5	6	7	8	9
10	11	12	13	14	15	16
17	18	19	20	21	22	23
24	25	26	27	28	29	30

October 2023

S	M	T	W	T	F	S
1	2	3	4	5	6	7
8	9	10	11	12	13	14
15	16	17	18	19	20	21
22	23	24	25	26	27	28
29	30	31				

NOTES

17 Sunday   Rosh Ha-Shanah   2

18 Monday   Fast of Gedaliah   3

19 Tuesday   4

20 Wednesday   5

21 Thursday   6

International Day of Peace

22 Friday   7

September 2023

S	M	T	W	T	F	S
					1	2
3	4	5	6	7	8	9
10	11	12	13	14	15	16
17	18	19	20	21	22	23
24	25	26	27	28	29	30

October 2023

S	M	T	W	T	F	S
1	2	3	4	5	6	7
8	9	10	11	12	13	14
15	16	17	18	19	20	21
22	23	24	25	26	27	28
29	30	31				

23 Saturday   Shabbat Shuva   8
                                                         Parashat Ha'Azinu

First Day of Autumn

SEPTEMBER 2023

24 Sunday Erev Yom Kippur 9

Yom Kippur (Begins at Sundown)

25 Monday Yom Kippur 10
Yizkor

26 Tuesday 11

27 Wednesday 12

28 Thursday 13

29 Friday Erev Sukkot 14

Full Moon

30 Saturday First Day of Sukkot 15

National Day for Truth and Reconciliation (Canada)

NOTES

September 2023

S	M	T	W	T	F	S
					1	2
3	4	5	6	7	8	9
10	11	12	13	14	15	16
17	18	19	20	21	22	23
24	25	26	27	28	29	30

October 2023

S	M	T	W	T	F	S
1	2	3	4	5	6	7
8	9	10	11	12	13	14
15	16	17	18	19	20	21
22	23	24	25	26	27	28
29	30	31				

THE JEWISH CALENDAR

2023–2024

THE JEWISH MUSEUM NEW YORK–5784

UNIVERSE

New Year Greeting. Germany, early 20th century. Embossed paper: printed and cut-out. 26.4 × 16.5 × 10.8 cm.
The Jewish Museum, New York. Gift of Mildred and George Weissman, 1999-9.

Torah Ark Curtain. Ottoman Empire, 18th century. Silk: embroidered with silk and metallic thread; appliqué with silk, spangles, and beads. 191 × 134 cm. The Jewish Museum, New York. Gift of Theresa Rosenberg, S 450.

Torah Case. Tunisia, 1832. Wood: carved, gessoed, painted, and gilt. 74 × 46 cm.
The Jewish Museum, New York. Gift of Judge Mayer Sulzberger, S 508.

OCTOBER 2023

S	M	T	W	T	F	S
1 16 TISHRI Second Day of Sukkot	**2** 17 TISHRI Hol ha-Mo-ed Sukkot	**3** 18 TISHRI Hol ha-Mo-ed Sukkot	**4** 19 TISHRI Hol ha-Mo-ed Sukkot	**5** 20 TISHRI Hol ha-Mo-ed Sukkot	**6** 21 TISHRI Hoshana Rabba	**7** 22 TISHRI Shemini Atzeret Yizkor
8 23 TISHRI Simhat Torah	**9** 24 TISHRI Columbus Day (US) Indigenous Peoples' Day (US) Thanksgiving Day (Canada)	**10** 25 TISHRI	**11** 26 TISHRI	**12** 27 TISHRI	**13** 28 TISHRI	**14** 29 TISHRI Shabbat Mevarekhim Parashat Bereshit
15 30 TISHRI Rosh Hodesh	**16** 1 HESHVAN Rosh Hodesh	**17** 2 HESHVAN	**18** 3 HESHVAN	**19** 4 HESHVAN	**20** 5 HESHVAN	**21** 6 HESHVAN Parashat No'ah
22 7 HESHVAN	**23** 8 HESHVAN	**24** 9 HESHVAN	**25** 10 HESHVAN	**26** 11 HESHVAN	**27** 12 HESHVAN	**28** 13 HESHVAN Full Moon Parashat Lekh Lekha
29 14 HESHVAN	**30** 15 HESHVAN	**31** 16 HESHVAN Halloween				

OCTOBER 2023

TISHRI 5784
תשרי

1	Sunday	Second Day of Sukkot	16
2	Monday	Hol ha-Mo-ed Sukkot	17
3	Tuesday	Hol ha-Mo-ed Sukkot	18
4	Wednesday	Hol ha-Mo-ed Sukkot	19
5	Thursday	Hol ha-Mo-ed Sukkot	20
6	Friday	Hoshana Rabba	21
7	Saturday	Shemini Atzeret Yizkor	22

NOTES

October 2023

S	M	T	W	T	F	S
1	2	3	4	5	6	7
8	9	10	11	12	13	14
15	16	17	18	19	20	21
22	23	24	25	26	27	28
29	30	31				

November 2023

S	M	T	W	T	F	S
			1	2	3	4
5	6	7	8	9	10	11
12	13	14	15	16	17	18
19	20	21	22	23	24	25
26	27	28	29	30		

Sukkah Model. *Dining Room with Walls as Projections of Chairs and Table (Study for Sukkah)*. Allan Wexler (American, b. 1949).
New York, United States, 1988. Basswood. 17.1 × 20.3 × 17.8 cm. The Jewish Museum, New York. Purchase: Judaica Acquisitions Fund, 1998-86.

Memorial Calendar. Yosef Yehudah Shore (American, b. Romania, d. 1919). Boston, United States, early 20th century. Watercolor on paper. 61 × 50.8 cm. The Jewish Museum, New York. Gift of Deborah Shore Kandler in memory of her father, Yosef Yehudah Shore, 1985–22.

OCTOBER 2023

NOTES

----

8 Sunday — Simhat Torah — **23**

9 Monday — **24**

Columbus Day (US)
Indigenous Peoples' Day (US)
Thanksgiving Day (Canada)

10 Tuesday — **25**

11 Wednesday — **26**

12 Thursday — **27**

13 Friday — **28**

14 Saturday — Shabbat Mevarekhim / Parashat Bereshit — **29**

October 2023

S	M	T	W	T	F	S
1	2	3	4	5	6	7
8	9	10	11	12	13	14
15	16	17	18	19	20	21
22	23	24	25	26	27	28
29	30	31				

November 2023

S	M	T	W	T	F	S
			1	2	3	4
5	6	7	8	9	10	11
12	13	14	15	16	17	18
19	20	21	22	23	24	25
26	27	28	29	30		

OCTOBER 2023

15	Sunday	Rosh Hodesh	30

NOTES

16	Monday	Rosh Hodesh	1

17	Tuesday	2

18	Wednesday	3

19	Thursday	4

20	Friday	5

October 2023

S	M	T	W	T	F	S
1	2	3	4	5	6	7
8	9	10	11	12	13	14
15	16	17	18	19	20	21
22	23	24	25	26	27	28
29	30	31				

21	Saturday	Parashat No'ah	6

November 2023

S	M	T	W	T	F	S
			1	2	3	4
5	6	7	8	9	10	11
12	13	14	15	16	17	18
19	20	21	22	23	24	25
26	27	28	29	30		

NOTES

| 22 Sunday | 7 |

| 23 Monday | 8 |

| 24 Tuesday | 9 |

| 25 Wednesday | 10 |

| 26 Thursday | 11 |

October 2023

S	M	T	W	T	F	S
1	2	3	4	5	6	7
8	9	10	11	12	13	14
15	16	17	18	19	20	21
22	23	24	25	26	27	28
29	30	31				

| 27 Friday | 12 |

November 2023

S	M	T	W	T	F	S
			1	2	3	4
5	6	7	8	9	10	11
12	13	14	15	16	17	18
19	20	21	22	23	24	25
26	27	28	29	30		

| 28 Saturday | Parashat Lekh Lekha | 13 |

Full Moon

Robe. *Djoma*. Samarkand (Uzbekistan), late 19th century. Silk: ikat; cotton: printed. 135.3 × 222.3 cm. The Jewish Museum, New York. Gift of Ben Zion Aron Bayof in memory of his father Rachamim ben Shalomo Aron-Bayof and his wife's father Yonah Niez Bayof, JM 216-68.

NOVEMBER 2023

S	M	T	W	T	F	S
			1 17 HESHVAN	**2** 18 HESHVAN	**3** 19 HESHVAN	**4** 20 HESHVAN *Parashat Vayera*
5 21 HESHVAN Daylight Saving Time Ends (US & Canada)	**6** 22 HESHVAN	**7** 23 HESHVAN Election Day (US)	**8** 24 HESHVAN	**9** 25 HESHVAN	**10** 26 HESHVAN	**11** 27 HESHVAN Veterans Day (US) Remembrance Day (Canada & UK) Shabbat Mevarekhim *Parashat Hayyei Sarah*
12 28 HESHVAN Remembrance Sunday (UK)	**13** 29 HESHVAN	**14** 1 KISLEV Rosh Hodesh	**15** 2 KISLEV	**16** 3 KISLEV	**17** 4 KISLEV	**18** 5 KISLEV *Parashat Toledot*
19 6 KISLEV	**20** 7 KISLEV	**21** 8 KISLEV	**22** 9 KISLEV	**23** 10 KISLEV Thanksgiving Day (US)	**24** 11 KISLEV	**25** 12 KISLEV *Parashat Vayeze*
26 13 KISLEV	**27** 14 KISLEV Full Moon	**28** 15 KISLEV	**29** 16 KISLEV	**30** 17 KISLEV		

OCTOBER / NOVEMBER 2023

HESHVAN 5784
חשון

29 Sunday	14

30 Monday	15

31 Tuesday	16

Halloween

1 Wednesday	17

2 Thursday	18

3 Friday	19

4 Saturday	Parashat Vayera	20

NOTES

October 2023

S	M	T	W	T	F	S
1	2	3	4	5	6	7
8	9	10	11	12	13	14
15	16	17	18	19	20	21
22	23	24	25	26	27	28
29	30	31				

November 2023

S	M	T	W	T	F	S
			1	2	3	4
5	6	7	8	9	10	11
12	13	14	15	16	17	18
19	20	21	22	23	24	25
26	27	28	29	30		

Sabbath Candlesticks. Moshe Zabari (Israeli, b. 1935). New York, United States, 1965. Nickel silver. Each: 30.5 × 8.3 × 9.5 cm.
The Jewish Museum, New York. Gift of the Abram and Frances Kanof Collection, JM 116-65a-b.

NOVEMBER 2023

5   Sunday   21

Daylight Saving Time Ends
(US & Canada)

6   Monday   22

7   Tuesday   23

Election Day (US)

8   Wednesday   24

9   Thursday   25

10   Friday   26

11   Saturday   Shabbat Mevarekhim   27
Parashat Hayyei Sarah

Veterans Day (US)

Remembrance Day
(Canada & UK)

NOTES

November 2023

S	M	T	W	T	F	S
			1	2	3	4
5	6	7	8	9	10	11
12	13	14	15	16	17	18
19	20	21	22	23	24	25
26	27	28	29	30		

December 2023

S	M	T	W	T	F	S
					1	2
3	4	5	6	7	8	9
10	11	12	13	14	15	16
17	18	19	20	21	22	23
24	25	26	27	28	29	30
31						

NOVEMBER 2023

NOTES

12 Sunday	28

Remembrance Sunday (UK)

13 Monday	29

14 Tuesday	Rosh Hodesh	1

15 Wednesday	2

16 Thursday	3

November 2023

S	M	T	W	T	F	S
			1	2	3	4
5	6	7	8	9	10	11
12	13	14	15	16	17	18
19	20	21	22	23	24	25
26	27	28	29	30		

17 Friday	4

December 2023

S	M	T	W	T	F	S
					1	2
3	4	5	6	7	8	9
10	11	12	13	14	15	16
17	18	19	20	21	22	23
24	25	26	27	28	29	30
31						

18 Saturday	Parashat Toledot	5

NOVEMBER 2023

19 Sunday	6

20 Monday	7

21 Tuesday	8

22 Wednesday	9

23 Thursday	10

Thanksgiving Day (US)

24 Friday	11

25 Saturday	Parashat Vayeze	12

NOTES

November 2023

S	M	T	W	T	F	S
			1	2	3	4
5	6	7	8	9	10	11
12	13	14	15	16	17	18
19	20	21	22	23	24	25
26	27	28	29	30		

December 2023

S	M	T	W	T	F	S
					1	2
3	4	5	6	7	8	9
10	11	12	13	14	15	16
17	18	19	20	21	22	23
24	25	26	27	28	29	30
31						

Quilt. Adolph Schermer (American, b. Austria-Hungary, 1846–1934). New York, United States, c. 1880–1900. Silk: appliquéd and pieced; cotton; satin backing. 168.9 × 188.6 cm. The Jewish Museum, New York. Gift of David B. and Irma L. Kroman, 1988-89.

Hanukkah Lamp. Netherlands (?), 19th century (?). Copper alloy: cast. 35.5 × 21.6 × 4.8 cm.
The Jewish Museum, New York. The Rose and Benjamin Mintz Collection, M 323.

DECEMBER 2023

S	M	T	W	T	F	S
					1 18 KISLEV	**2** 19 KISLEV
						Parashat Vayishlah
3 20 KISLEV	**4** 21 KISLEV	**5** 22 KISLEV	**6** 23 KISLEV	**7** 24 KISLEV Hanukkah (Begins at Sundown) Erev Hanukkah	**8** 25 KISLEV First Day of Hanukkah	**9** 26 KISLEV Shabbat Mevarekhim Parashat Vayeshev Second Day of Hanukkah
10 27 KISLEV Human Rights Day Third Day of Hanukkah	**11** 28 KISLEV Fourth Day of Hanukkah	**12** 29 KISLEV Fifth Day of Hanukkah	**13** 1 TEVET Rosh Hodesh Sixth Day of Hanukkah	**14** 2 TEVET Seventh Day of Hanukkah	**15** 3 TEVET Eighth Day of Hanukkah	**16** 4 TEVET Parashat Mi-kez
17 5 TEVET	**18** 6 TEVET	**19** 7 TEVET	**20** 8 TEVET	**21** 9 TEVET First Day of Winter	**22** 10 TEVET	**23** 11 TEVET Parashat Vayiggash
24 12 TEVET	**25** 13 TEVET Christmas	**26** 14 TEVET Kwanzaa Begins Boxing Day (Canada & UK) Full Moon	**27** 15 TEVET	**28** 16 TEVET	**29** 17 TEVET	**30** 18 TEVET
19 TEVET **31**						Parashat Vayehi

26 Sunday		13

NOTES

27 Monday		14

Full Moon

28 Tuesday		15

29 Wednesday		16

30 Thursday		17

1 Friday		18

2 Saturday	*Parashat Vayishlah*	19

November 2023

S	M	T	W	T	F	S
			1	2	3	4
5	6	7	8	9	10	11
12	13	14	15	16	17	18
19	20	21	22	23	24	25
26	27	28	29	30		

December 2023

S	M	T	W	T	F	S
					1	2
3	4	5	6	7	8	9
10	11	12	13	14	15	16
17	18	19	20	21	22	23
24	25	26	27	28	29	30
31						

NOTES

3 Sunday 20

---

4 Monday 21

---

5 Tuesday 22

---

6 Wednesday 23

---

7 Thursday Erev Hanukkah 24

December 2023

S	M	T	W	T	F	S
					1	2
3	4	5	6	7	8	9
10	11	12	13	14	15	16
17	18	19	20	21	22	23
24	25	26	27	28	29	30
31						

Hanukkah (Begins at Sundown)

8 Friday First Day of Hanukkah 25

January 2024

S	M	T	W	T	F	S
	1	2	3	4	5	6
7	8	9	10	11	12	13
14	15	16	17	18	19	20
21	22	23	24	25	26	27
28	29	30	31			

9 Saturday Shabbat Mevarekhim 26
Parashat Vayeshev
Second Day of Hanukkah

DECEMBER 2023

10	Sunday	Third Day of Hanukkah	27

Human Rights Day

11	Monday	Fourth Day of Hanukkah	28

12	Tuesday	Fifth Day of Hanukkah	29

13	Wednesday	Rosh Hodesh Sixth Day of Hanukkah	1

14	Thursday	Seventh Day of Hanukkah	2

15	Friday	Eighth Day of Hanukkah	3

16	Saturday	Parashat Mi-kez	4

NOTES

December 2023

S	M	T	W	T	F	S
					1	2
3	4	5	6	7	8	9
10	11	12	13	14	15	16
17	18	19	20	21	22	23
24	25	26	27	28	29	30
31						

January 2024

S	M	T	W	T	F	S
	1	2	3	4	5	6
7	8	9	10	11	12	13
14	15	16	17	18	19	20
21	22	23	24	25	26	27
28	29	30	31			

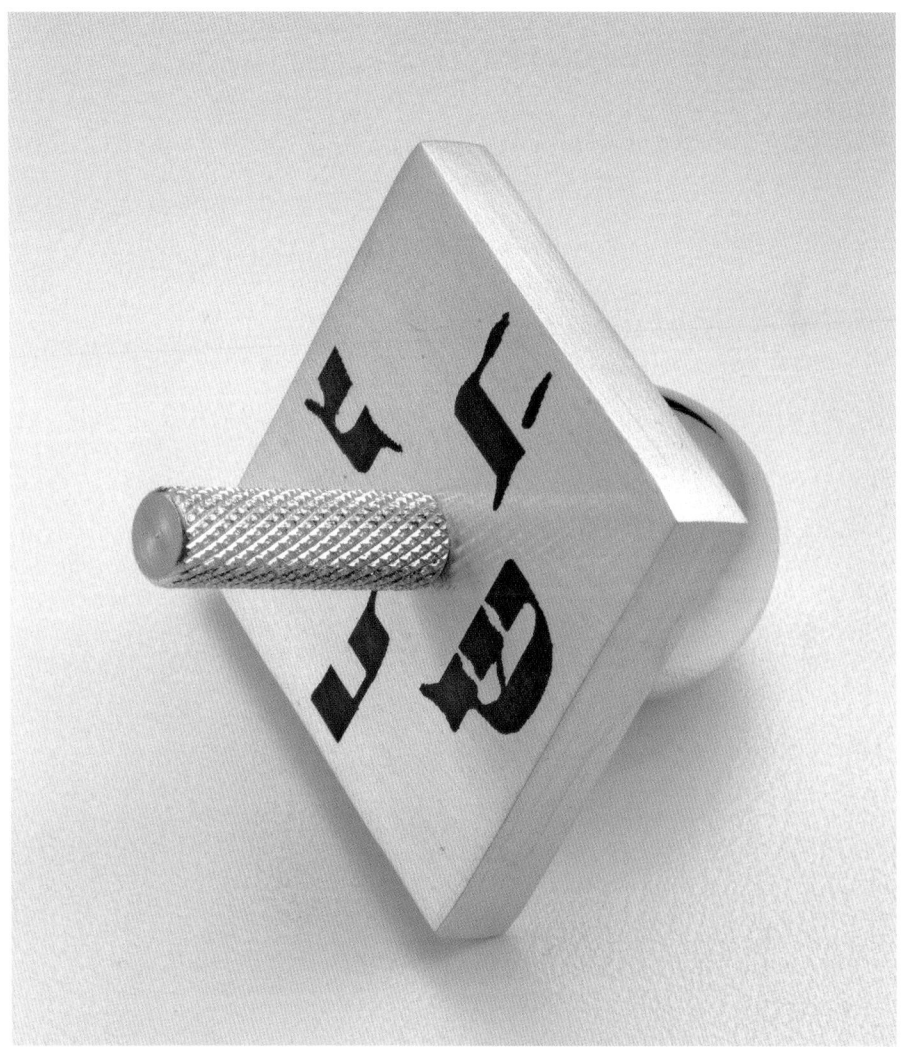

Dreidel. *Executive Dreidel*. Michael Berkowicz (Polish, b. Russia, 1944). Bonnie Srolovitz-Berkowicz (American, b. 1955).
New York, United States, 1993. Brass: silver-plated and painted. 5.1 × 3.8 × 3.8 cm.
The Jewish Museum, New York. Purchase: Judaica Acquisitions Fund, 1993-248.

DECEMBER 2023

17	Sunday	5

18	Monday	6

19	Tuesday	7

20	Wednesday	8

21	Thursday	9

First Day of Winter

22	Friday	10

23	Saturday	Parashat Vayiggash	11

NOTES

December 2023

S	M	T	W	T	F	S
					1	2
3	4	5	6	7	8	9
10	11	12	13	14	15	16
17	18	19	20	21	22	23
24	25	26	27	28	29	30
31						

January 2024

S	M	T	W	T	F	S
	1	2	3	4	5	6
7	8	9	10	11	12	13
14	15	16	17	18	19	20
21	22	23	24	25	26	27
28	29	30	31			

NOTES

---

24 Sunday   12

---

25 Monday   13

Christmas

---

26 Tuesday   14

Kwanzaa Begins
Boxing Day (Canada & UK)
Full Moon

---

27 Wednesday   15

---

28 Thursday   16

December 2023

S	M	T	W	T	F	S
					1	2
3	4	5	6	7	8	9
10	11	12	13	14	15	16
17	18	19	20	21	22	23
24	25	26	27	28	29	30
31						

29 Friday   17

January 2024

S	M	T	W	T	F	S
	1	2	3	4	5	6
7	8	9	10	11	12	13
14	15	16	17	18	19	20
21	22	23	24	25	26	27
28	29	30	31			

30 Saturday   Parashat Vayehi   18

Clock. Probably Philipp Happacher (German, 1784–1843). Vienna (Austria), c. 1818–43. Copper alloy: silvered, cast, chased, and engraved. 17.1 × 12.9 × 7 cm. The Jewish Museum, New York. Bequest of Elizabeth Cats in memory of her father Leopold Silberstein, 1997-144a-b.

JANUARY 2024

S	M	T	W	T	F	S
	1 20 TEVET New Year's Day	**2** 21 TEVET	**3** 22 TEVET	**4** 23 TEVET	**5** 24 TEVET	**6** 25 TEVET Shabbat Mevarekhim Parashat Shemot
7 26 TEVET	**8** 27 TEVET	**9** 28 TEVET	**10** 29 TEVET	**11** 1 SHEVAT Rosh Hodesh	**12** 2 SHEVAT	**13** 3 SHEVAT Parashat Va-era
14 4 SHEVAT	**15** 5 SHEVAT Martin Luther King Jr. Day (US)	**16** 6 SHEVAT	**17** 7 SHEVAT	**18** 8 SHEVAT	**19** 9 SHEVAT	**20** 10 SHEVAT Parashat Bo
21 11 SHEVAT	**22** 12 SHEVAT	**23** 13 SHEVAT	**24** 14 SHEVAT	**25** 15 SHEVAT Full Moon Tu Bishvat	**26** 16 SHEVAT	**27** 17 SHEVAT International Holocaust Remembrance Day Shabbat Shirah Parashat Beshalach
28 18 SHEVAT	**29** 19 SHEVAT	**30** 20 SHEVAT	**31** 21 SHEVAT			

DECEMBER 2023 / JANUARY 2024

TEVET 5784

טבת

31	Sunday	19

1	Monday	20

New Year's Day

2	Tuesday	21

3	Wednesday	22

4	Thursday	23

5	Friday	24

6	Saturday	Shabbat Mevarekhim Parashat Shemot	25

NOTES

January 2024

S	M	T	W	T	F	S
	1	2	3	4	5	6
7	8	9	10	11	12	13
14	15	16	17	18	19	20
21	22	23	24	25	26	27
28	29	30	31			

February 2024

S	M	T	W	T	F	S
				1	2	3
4	5	6	7	8	9	10
11	12	13	14	15	16	17
18	19	20	21	22	23	24
25	26	27	28	29		

JANUARY 2024

NOTES

_____
_____
_____
_____
_____
_____
_____
_____
_____
_____
_____
_____
_____
_____
_____
_____

7 Sunday 26

8 Monday 27

9 Tuesday 28

10 Wednesday 29

11 Thursday Rosh Hodesh 1

12 Friday 2

13 Saturday Parashat Va-era 3

January 2024

S	M	T	W	T	F	S
	1	2	3	4	5	6
7	8	9	10	11	12	13
14	15	16	17	18	19	20
21	22	23	24	25	26	27
28	29	30	31			

February 2024

S	M	T	W	T	F	S
				1	2	3
4	5	6	7	8	9	10
11	12	13	14	15	16	17
18	19	20	21	22	23	24
25	26	27	28	29		

JANUARY 2024

14 Sunday   4

15 Monday   5

Martin Luther King Jr. Day (US)

16 Tuesday   6

17 Wednesday   7

18 Thursday   8

19 Friday   9

20 Saturday   Parashat Bo   10

NOTES

January 2024

S	M	T	W	T	F	S
	1	2	3	4	5	6
7	8	9	10	11	12	13
14	15	16	17	18	19	20
21	22	23	24	25	26	27
28	29	30	31			

February 2024

S	M	T	W	T	F	S
				1	2	3
4	5	6	7	8	9	10
11	12	13	14	15	16	17
18	19	20	21	22	23	24
25	26	27	28	29		

NOTES

21 Sunday   11

22 Monday   12

23 Tuesday   13

24 Wednesday   14

25 Thursday   Tu Bishvat   15

Full Moon

26 Friday   16

27 Saturday   Shabbat Shirah   17
Parashat Beshalach

International Holocaust Remembrance Day

January 2024

S	M	T	W	T	F	S
	1	2	3	4	5	6
7	8	9	10	11	12	13
14	15	16	17	18	19	20
21	22	23	24	25	26	27
28	29	30	31			

February 2024

S	M	T	W	T	F	S
				1	2	3
4	5	6	7	8	9	10
11	12	13	14	15	16	17
18	19	20	21	22	23	24
25	26	27	28	29		

Alms Container. *Masinekele—Let us Give.* Jeremiah Maloi (South African, b. 1969). Monkeybiz (South African).
Cape Town, South Africa, 2007. Glass beads: woven. Central group: 41.3 × 24.4 × 10.5 cm. The Jewish Museum, New York.
Purchase: Sanford C. Bernstein Foundation Fund and Contemporary Judaica Acquisitions Committee Fund, 2007-16a-d.

FEBRUARY 2024

S	M	T	W	T	F	S
				1 22 SHEVAT	**2** 23 SHEVAT	**3** 24 SHEVAT
					Groundhog Day	Shabbat Mevarekhim Parashat Yitro
4 25 SHEVAT	**5** 26 SHEVAT	**6** 27 SHEVAT	**7** 28 SHEVAT	**8** 29 SHEVAT	**9** 30 SHEVAT	**10** 1 ADAR I
					Rosh Hodesh	Lunar New Year Rosh Hodesh Parashat Mishpatim
11 2 ADAR I	**12** 3 ADAR I	**13** 4 ADAR I	**14** 5 ADAR I	**15** 6 ADAR I	**16** 7 ADAR I	**17** 8 ADAR I
			Valentine's Day Ash Wednesday			Parashat Terumah
18 9 ADAR I	**19** 10 ADAR I	**20** 11 ADAR I	**21** 12 ADAR I	**22** 13 ADAR I	**23** 14 ADAR I	**24** 15 ADAR I
	Presidents' Day (US)					Full Moon Parashat Tezavveh
25 16 ADAR I	**26** 17 ADAR I	**27** 18 ADAR I	**28** 19 ADAR I	**29** 20 ADAR I		

JANUARY / FEBRUARY 2024

28 Sunday		18

NOTES

29 Monday		19

30 Tuesday		20

31 Wednesday		21

1 Thursday		22

2 Friday		23

January 2024

S	M	T	W	T	F	S
	1	2	3	4	5	6
7	8	9	10	11	12	13
14	15	16	17	18	19	20
21	22	23	24	25	26	27
28	29	30	31			

Groundhog Day

3 Saturday	Shabbat Mevarekhim Parashat Yitro	24

February 2024

S	M	T	W	T	F	S
				1	2	3
4	5	6	7	8	9	10
11	12	13	14	15	16	17
18	19	20	21	22	23	24
25	26	27	28	29		

FEBRUARY 2024

SHEVAT / ADAR I 5784

שבט / אדר א

4	Sunday	25
5	Monday	26
6	Tuesday	27
7	Wednesday	28
8	Thursday	29
9	Friday	Rosh Hodesh 30
10	Saturday	Rosh Hodesh 1 Parashat Mishpatim

Lunar New Year

NOTES

February 2024

S	M	T	W	T	F	S
				1	2	3
4	5	6	7	8	9	10
11	12	13	14	15	16	17
18	19	20	21	22	23	24
25	26	27	28	29		

March 2024

S	M	T	W	T	F	S
					1	2
3	4	5	6	7	8	9
10	11	12	13	14	15	16
17	18	19	20	21	22	23
24	25	26	27	28	29	30
31						

FEBRUARY 2024

11 Sunday 2

12 Monday 3

13 Tuesday 4

14 Wednesday 5

Valentine's Day
Ash Wednesday

15 Thursday 6

16 Friday 7

17 Saturday Parashat Terumah 8

NOTES

February 2024

S	M	T	W	T	F	S
				1	2	3
4	5	6	7	8	9	10
11	12	13	14	15	16	17
18	19	20	21	22	23	24
25	26	27	28	29		

March 2024

S	M	T	W	T	F	S
					1	2
3	4	5	6	7	8	9
10	11	12	13	14	15	16
17	18	19	20	21	22	23
24	25	26	27	28	29	30
31						

18	Sunday	9

_____

_____

19 Monday · 10

_____

_____

_____

_____

Presidents' Day (US)

20 Tuesday · 11

_____

_____

_____

_____

21 Wednesday · 12

_____

_____

_____

22 Thursday · 13

_____

February 2024

S	M	T	W	T	F	S
				1	2	3
4	5	6	7	8	9	10
11	12	13	14	15	16	17
18	19	20	21	22	23	24
25	26	27	28	29		

23 Friday · 14

March 2024

S	M	T	W	T	F	S
					1	2
3	4	5	6	7	8	9
10	11	12	13	14	15	16
17	18	19	20	21	22	23
24	25	26	27	28	29	30
31						

24 Saturday · Parashat Tezavveh · 15

Full Moon

Esther Scroll in Case. Case: United States (?). 1912 (date of inscription). Silver: traced, engraved, cast; glass; ink on parchment. 31.8 × 6.4 × 4.8 cm. The Jewish Museum, New York. Gift of Dr. Harry G. Friedman, F 4601a-b.

MARCH 2024

S	M	T	W	T	F	S
					1 21 ADAR I	**2** 22 ADAR I Parashat Ki Tissa
3 23 ADAR I	**4** 24 ADAR I	**5** 25 ADAR I	**6** 26 ADAR I	**7** 27 ADAR I	**8** 28 ADAR I International Women's Day	**9** 29 ADAR I Shabbat Shekalim Shabbat Mevarekhim Parashat Vayakhel
10 30 ADAR I Daylight Saving Time Begins (US & Canada) Rosh Hodesh	**11** 1 ADAR II Rosh Hodesh	**12** 2 ADAR II	**13** 3 ADAR II	**14** 4 ADAR II	**15** 5 ADAR II	**16** 6 ADAR II Parashat Pekudei
17 7 ADAR II St. Patrick's Day	**18** 8 ADAR II	**19** 9 ADAR II First Day of Spring	**20** 10 ADAR II	**21** 11 ADAR II Fast of Esther	**22** 12 ADAR II	**23** 13 ADAR II Shabbat Zakhor Parashat Vayikra Erev Purim
24 14 ADAR II Palm Sunday Purim 21 ADAR II Easter **31**	**25** 15 ADAR II Full Moon Shushan Purim	**26** 16 ADAR II	**27** 17 ADAR II	**28** 18 ADAR II	**29** 19 ADAR II Good Friday	**30** 20 ADAR II Shabbat Parah Parashat Zav

25 Sunday 16

26 Monday 17

27 Tuesday 18

28 Wednesday 19

29 Thursday 20

1 Friday 21

2 Saturday — Parashat Ki Tissa — 22

NOTES

_____
_____
_____
_____
_____
_____
_____
_____
_____
_____
_____
_____
_____
_____
_____
_____
_____
_____

February 2024

S	M	T	W	T	F	S
				1	2	3
4	5	6	7	8	9	10
11	12	13	14	15	16	17
18	19	20	21	22	23	24
25	26	27	28	29		

March 2024

S	M	T	W	T	F	S
					1	2
3	4	5	6	7	8	9
10	11	12	13	14	15	16
17	18	19	20	21	22	23
24	25	26	27	28	29	30
31						

NOTES		
	3 Sunday	23
	4 Monday	24
	5 Tuesday	25
	6 Wednesday	26
	7 Thursday	27

February 2024

S	M	T	W	T	F	S
				1	2	3
4	5	6	7	8	9	10
11	12	13	14	15	16	17
18	19	20	21	22	23	24
25	26	27	28	29		

8 Friday — 28

International Women's Day

March 2024

S	M	T	W	T	F	S
					1	2
3	4	5	6	7	8	9
10	11	12	13	14	15	16
17	18	19	20	21	22	23
24	25	26	27	28	29	30
31						

9 Saturday

Shabbat Shekalim
Shabbat Mevarekhim
Parashat Vayakhel

29

MARCH 2024

10 Sunday   Rosh Hodesh   **30**

Daylight Saving Time Begins
(US & Canada)

11 Monday   Rosh Hodesh   **1**

12 Tuesday   **2**

13 Wednesday   **3**

14 Thursday   **4**

15 Friday   **5**

16 Saturday   -   Parashat Pekudei **6**

NOTES

March 2024

S	M	T	W	T	F	S
					1	2
3	4	5	6	7	8	9
10	11	12	13	14	15	16
17	18	19	20	21	22	23
24	25	26	27	28	29	30
31						

April 2024

S	M	T	W	T	F	S
	1	2	3	4	5	6
7	8	9	10	11	12	13
14	15	16	17	18	19	20
21	22	23	24	25	26	27
28	29	30				

Kiddush Cup. Lella Vignelli (American, b. Italy, 1934–2016), Vignelli Designs. Manufacturer: San Lorenzo srl. Milan, Italy, 2007.
Silver: handworked. Height: 14 cm, Diameter: 8.1 cm. The Jewish Museum, New York.
Purchase: Contemporary Judaica Acquisitions Committee and Tobe Pascher Workshop Funds, 2008-35.

17	Sunday	7

St. Patrick's Day

18	Monday	8

19	Tuesday	9

First Day of Spring

20	Wednesday	10

21	Thursday	Fast of Esther	11

22	Friday	12

23	Saturday	Shabbat Zakhor	13
		Parashat Vayikra	
		Erev Purim	

NOTES

March 2024

S	M	T	W	T	F	S
					1	2
3	4	5	6	7	8	9
10	11	12	13	14	15	16
17	18	19	20	21	22	23
24	25	26	27	28	29	30
31						

April 2024

S	M	T	W	T	F	S
	1	2	3	4	5	6
7	8	9	10	11	12	13
14	15	16	17	18	19	20
21	22	23	24	25	26	27
28	29	30				

MARCH 2024

NOTES

_____
_____
_____
_____
_____
_____
_____
_____
_____
_____
_____
_____
_____
_____
_____
_____

24 Sunday — Purim **14**

Palm Sunday

25 Monday — Shushan Purim **15**

Full Moon

26 Tuesday **16**

27 Wednesday **17**

28 Thursday **18**

29 Friday **19**

Good Friday

30 Saturday — Shabbat Parah / Parashat Zav **20**

March 2024

S	M	T	W	T	F	S
					1	2
3	4	5	6	7	8	9
10	11	12	13	14	15	16
17	18	19	20	21	22	23
24	25	26	27	28	29	30
31						

April 2024

S	M	T	W	T	F	S
	1	2	3	4	5	6
7	8	9	10	11	12	13
14	15	16	17	18	19	20
21	22	23	24	25	26	27
28	29	30				

Seder Plate. Nicole Eisenman (American, b. France, 1965). United States, 2015. Ceramic: painted. Diameter: 36 cm. The Jewish Museum, New York. Commission: Dr. Joel and Phyllis Gitlin Judaica Acquisitions Fund, Contemporary Judaica Acquisitions Interest Fund, and Alex Schmelzer and Lisa Rotmil Gift, 2015-5.

APRIL 2024

S	M	T	W	T	F	S
	1 22 ADAR II Easter Monday (Canada & UK)	**2** 23 ADAR II	**3** 24 ADAR II	**4** 25 ADAR II	**5** 26 ADAR II	**6** 27 ADAR II Shabbat Ha Hodesh Shabbat Mevarekhim Parashat Shemini
7 28 ADAR II	**8** 29 ADAR II	**9** 1 NISAN Rosh Hodesh	**10** 2 NISAN	**11** 3 NISAN	**12** 4 NISAN	**13** 5 NISAN Parashat Tazria
14 6 NISAN	**15** 7 NISAN	**16** 8 NISAN	**17** 9 NISAN	**18** 10 NISAN	**19** 11 NISAN	**20** 12 NISAN Shabbat Hagadol Parashat Mezora
21 13 NISAN	**22** 14 NISAN Earth Day Passover (Begins at Sundown) Erev Pesah	**23** 15 NISAN **Full Moon** First Day of Pesah	**24** 16 NISAN Second Day of Pesah Sefirat ha-Omer begins	**25** 17 NISAN Hol ha-Mo-ed Pesah	**26** 18 NISAN Hol ha-Mo-ed Pesah	**27** 19 NISAN Hol ha-Mo-ed Pesah
28 20 NISAN Hol ha-Mo-ed Pesah	**29** 21 NISAN Seventh Day of Pesah	**30** 22 NISAN Eighth Day of Pesah Yizkor				

MARCH / APRIL 2024

ADAR II 5784

אדר ב

31	Sunday	21

Easter

1	Monday	22

Easter Monday (Canada & UK)

2	Tuesday	23

3	Wednesday	24

4	Thursday	25

5	Friday	26

6	Saturday	Shabbat Ha Hodesh Shabbat Mevarekhim Parashat Shemini	27

NOTES

April 2024

S	M	T	W	T	F	S
	1	2	3	4	5	6
7	8	9	10	11	12	13
14	15	16	17	18	19	20
21	22	23	24	25	26	27
28	29	30				

May 2024

S	M	T	W	T	F	S
			1	2	3	4
5	6	7	8	9	10	11
12	13	14	15	16	17	18
19	20	21	22	23	24	25
26	27	28	29	30	31	

Hanging Lamp Fragment. North Africa, 19th century. Copper alloy: cast and engraved; enamel. 18 × 12.2 cm. The Jewish Museum, New York. Gift of Dr. Harry G. Friedman, F 2977.

APRIL 2024

7	Sunday		28

8	Monday		29

9	Tuesday	Rosh Hodesh	1

10	Wednesday		2

11	Thursday		3

12	Friday		4

13	Saturday	Parashat Tazria	5

NOTES

April 2024

S	M	T	W	T	F	S
	1	2	3	4	5	6
7	8	9	10	11	12	13
14	15	16	17	18	19	20
21	22	23	24	25	26	27
28	29	30				

May 2024

S	M	T	W	T	F	S
			1	2	3	4
5	6	7	8	9	10	11
12	13	14	15	16	17	18
19	20	21	22	23	24	25
26	27	28	29	30	31	

NOTES

14 Sunday   6

_____
_____
_____
_____
_____

15 Monday   7

_____
_____
_____

16 Tuesday   8

_____
_____
_____
_____

17 Wednesday   9

_____
_____
_____

18 Thursday   10

April 2024

S	M	T	W	T	F	S
	1	2	3	4	5	6
7	8	9	10	11	12	13
14	15	16	17	18	19	20
21	22	23	24	25	26	27
28	29	30				

19 Friday   11

May 2024

S	M	T	W	T	F	S
			1	2	3	4
5	6	7	8	9	10	11
12	13	14	15	16	17	18
19	20	21	22	23	24	25
26	27	28	29	30	31	

20 Saturday   Shabbat Hagadol   12
Parashat Mezora

APRIL 2024

21	Sunday		13

NOTES

22	Monday	Erev Pesah	14

Earth Day
Passover (Begins at Sundown)

23	Tuesday	First Day of Pesah	15

Full Moon

24	Wednesday	Second Day of Pesah	16
		Sefirat ha-Omer begins	

25	Thursday	Hol ha-Mo-ed Pesah	17

26	Friday	Hol ha-Mo-ed Pesah	18

April 2024

S	M	T	W	T	F	S
	1	2	3	4	5	6
7	8	9	10	11	12	13
14	15	16	17	18	19	20
21	22	23	24	25	26	27
28	29	30				

27	Saturday	Hol ha-Mo-ed Pesah	19

May 2024

S	M	T	W	T	F	S
			1	2	3	4
5	6	7	8	9	10	11
12	13	14	15	16	17	18
19	20	21	22	23	24	25
26	27	28	29	30	31	

Matzah Cover. Anni Albers (American, b. Germany, 1899–1994). United States, 1959.
Bast fiber and metallic threads; metallic cellophane. 41 × 42.2 cm. The Jewish Museum, New York.
Gift of Elaine Lustig Cohen, 2021-63. © The Josef and Anni Albers Foundation / Artists Rights Society (ARS), New York, 2022.

Carousel Horse. Charles Carmel (American, b. Russia, 1865–1931). United States, c. 1914. Carved and painted poplar wood and horsehair.
155 x 162.5 x 28 cm. The Jewish Museum, New York. Gift of Larry and Gail Freels, 2020-62.

MAY 2024

S	M	T	W	T	F	S
			1 23 NISAN	**2** 24 NISAN	**3** 25 NISAN	**4** 26 NISAN Shabbat Mevarekhim Parashat Aharei Mot
5 27 NISAN Orthodox Easter	**6** 28 NISAN Early May Bank Holiday (UK) Yom ha-Sho'ah	**7** 29 NISAN	**8** 30 NISAN Rosh Hodesh	**9** 1 IYYAR Rosh Hodesh	**10** 2 IYYAR	**11** 3 IYYAR Parashat Kedoshim
12 4 IYYAR Mother's Day	**13** 5 IYYAR Yom ha-Zikkaron	**14** 6 IYYAR Yom ha-Azma'ut	**15** 7 IYYAR	**16** 8 IYYAR	**17** 9 IYYAR	**18** 10 IYYAR Parashat Emor
19 11 IYYAR	**20** 12 IYYAR Victoria Day (Canada)	**21** 13 IYYAR	**22** 14 IYYAR	**23** 15 IYYAR Full Moon	**24** 16 IYYAR	**25** 17 IYYAR Parashat Behar
26 18 IYYAR Lag ba-Omer	**27** 19 IYYAR Memorial Day (US) Spring Bank Holiday (UK)	**28** 20 IYYAR	**29** 21 IYYAR	**30** 22 IYYAR	**31** 23 IYYAR	

| 28 | Sunday | Hol ha-Mo-ed Pesah | 20 |

NOTES

| 29 | Monday | Seventh Day of Pesah | 21 |

| 30 | Tuesday | Eighth Day of Pesah
Yizkor | 22 |

| 1 | Wednesday | | 23 |

| 2 | Thursday | | 24 |

| 3 | Friday | | 25 |

May 2024

S	M	T	W	T	F	S
			1	2	3	4
5	6	7	8	9	10	11
12	13	14	15	16	17	18
19	20	21	22	23	24	25
26	27	28	29	30	31	

| 4 | Saturday | Shabbat Mevarekhim
Parashat Aharei Mot | 26 |

June 2024

S	M	T	W	T	F	S
						1
2	3	4	5	6	7	8
9	10	11	12	13	14	15
16	17	18	19	20	21	22
23	24	25	26	27	28	29
30						

MAY 2024

NOTES

5 Sunday   27

Orthodox Easter

6 Monday   Yom ha-Sho'ah   28

Early May Bank Holiday (UK)

7 Tuesday   29

8 Wednesday   Rosh Hodesh   30

9 Thursday   Rosh Hodesh   1

10 Friday   2

11 Saturday   Parashat Kedoshim   3

May 2024

S	M	T	W	T	F	S
			1	2	3	4
5	6	7	8	9	10	11
12	13	14	15	16	17	18
19	20	21	22	23	24	25
26	27	28	29	30	31	

June 2024

S	M	T	W	T	F	S
						1
2	3	4	5	6	7	8
9	10	11	12	13	14	15
16	17	18	19	20	21	22
23	24	25	26	27	28	29
30						

MAY 2024

12	Sunday	4

Mother's Day

13	Monday	Yom ha-Zikkaron	5

14	Tuesday	Yom ha-Azma'ut	6

15	Wednesday	7

16	Thursday	8

17	Friday	9

18	Saturday	Parashat Emor	10

NOTES

May 2024

S	M	T	W	T	F	S
			1	2	3	4
5	6	7	8	9	10	11
12	13	14	15	16	17	18
19	20	21	22	23	24	25
26	27	28	29	30	31	

June 2024

S	M	T	W	T	F	S
						1
2	3	4	5	6	7	8
9	10	11	12	13	14	15
16	17	18	19	20	21	22
23	24	25	26	27	28	29
30						

NOTES

19 Sunday 11

20 Monday 12

Victoria Day (Canada)

21 Tuesday 13

22 Wednesday 14

23 Thursday 15

Full Moon

24 Friday 16

May 2024

S	M	T	W	T	F	S
			1	2	3	4
5	6	7	8	9	10	11
12	13	14	15	16	17	18
19	20	21	22	23	24	25
26	27	28	29	30	31	

June 2024

S	M	T	W	T	F	S
						1
2	3	4	5	6	7	8
9	10	11	12	13	14	15
16	17	18	19	20	21	22
23	24	25	26	27	28	29
30						

25 Saturday Parashat Behar 17

Spice Container. Kathe Berl (American, b. Austria, 1908–1994). New York, United States, 1964. Silver and enamel.
18.7 × 5.1 × 1.9 cm. The Jewish Museum, New York. Gift of Karl Nathan, JM 96-64.

JUNE 2024

S	M	T	W	T	F	S
						1 24 IYYAR Shabbat Mevarekhim Parashat Bechukotai
2 25 IYYAR	**3** 26 IYYAR	**4** 27 IYYAR	**5** 28 IYYAR Yom Yerushalayim	**6** 29 IYYAR	**7** 1 SIVAN Rosh Hodesh	**8** 2 SIVAN Parashat Bamidbar
9 3 SIVAN	**10** 4 SIVAN	**11** 5 SIVAN Erev Shavuot	**12** 6 SIVAN Shavuot	**13** 7 SIVAN Shavuot Yizkor	**14** 8 SIVAN	**15** 9 SIVAN Parashat Naso
16 10 SIVAN Father's Day	**17** 11 SIVAN	**18** 12 SIVAN	**19** 13 SIVAN Juneteenth National Independence Day (US)	**20** 14 SIVAN First Day of Summer	**21** 15 SIVAN Full Moon	**22** 16 SIVAN Parashat Be-ha'alotekha
23 17 SIVAN	**24** 18 SIVAN	**25** 19 SIVAN	**26** 20 SIVAN	**27** 21 SIVAN	**28** 22 SIVAN	**29** 23 SIVAN Shabbat Mevarekhim Parashat Shelah
24 SIVAN **30**						

MAY / JUNE 2024

26	Sunday	Lag ba-Omer	**18**

NOTES

27	Monday	**19**

Memorial Day (US)
Spring Bank Holiday (UK)

28	Tuesday	**20**

29	Wednesday	**21**

30	Thursday	**22**

31	Friday	**23**

1	Saturday	Shabbat Mevarekhim Parashat Bechukotai	**24**

May 2024

S	M	T	W	T	F	S
			1	2	3	4
5	6	7	8	9	10	11
12	13	14	15	16	17	18
19	20	21	22	23	24	25
26	27	28	29	30	31	

June 2024

S	M	T	W	T	F	S
						1
2	3	4	5	6	7	8
9	10	11	12	13	14	15
16	17	18	19	20	21	22
23	24	25	26	27	28	29
30						

NOTES

_____
_____
_____
_____
_____
_____
_____
_____
_____
_____
_____
_____
_____
_____
_____
_____
_____
_____
_____

2 Sunday · 25

3 Monday · 26

4 Tuesday · 27

5 Wednesday · · · · · · · · Yom Yerushalayim 28

6 Thursday · 29

June 2024

S	M	T	W	T	F	S
						1
2	3	4	5	6	7	8
9	10	11	12	13	14	15
16	17	18	19	20	21	22
23	24	25	26	27	28	29
30						

7 Friday · · · · · · · · · · · · · · · · Rosh Hodesh 1

July 2024

S	M	T	W	T	F	S
	1	2	3	4	5	6
7	8	9	10	11	12	13
14	15	16	17	18	19	20
21	22	23	24	25	26	27
28	29	30	31			

8 Saturday · · · · · · · · · · Parashat Bamidbar 2

JUNE 2024

סיון

9	Sunday		3

10	Monday		4

11	Tuesday	Erev Shavuot	5

12	Wednesday	Shavuot	6

13	Thursday	Shavuot Yizkor	7

14	Friday		8

15	Saturday	Parashat Naso	9

NOTES

June 2024

S	M	T	W	T	F	S
						1
2	3	4	5	6	7	8
9	10	11	12	13	14	15
16	17	18	19	20	21	22
23	24	25	26	27	28	29
30						

July 2024

S	M	T	W	T	F	S
	1	2	3	4	5	6
7	8	9	10	11	12	13
14	15	16	17	18	19	20
21	22	23	24	25	26	27
28	29	30	31			

NOTES

16 Sunday   10

_____
_____
_____
_____
_____

Father's Day

17 Monday   11

_____
_____
_____

18 Tuesday   12

_____
_____
_____
_____
_____

19 Wednesday   13

_____
_____

Juneteenth National Independence Day (US)

20 Thursday   14

_____
_____

June 2024

S	M	T	W	T	F	S
						1
2	3	4	5	6	7	8
9	10	11	12	13	14	15
16	17	18	19	20	21	22
23	24	25	26	27	28	29
30						

First Day of Summer

21 Friday   15

July 2024

S	M	T	W	T	F	S
	1	2	3	4	5	6
7	8	9	10	11	12	13
14	15	16	17	18	19	20
21	22	23	24	25	26	27
28	29	30	31			

Full Moon

22 Saturday   Parashat Be-ha'alotekha   16

JUNE 2024

23 Sunday		17
24 Monday		18
25 Tuesday		19
26 Wednesday		20
27 Thursday		21
28 Friday		22
29 Saturday	Shabbat Mevarekhim Parashat Shelah	23

NOTES

_____
_____
_____
_____
_____
_____
_____
_____
_____
_____
_____
_____
_____
_____
_____
_____
_____
_____

June 2024

S	M	T	W	T	F	S
						1
2	3	4	5	6	7	8
9	10	11	12	13	14	15
16	17	18	19	20	21	22
23	24	25	26	27	28	29
30						

July 2024

S	M	T	W	T	F	S
	1	2	3	4	5	6
7	8	9	10	11	12	13
14	15	16	17	18	19	20
21	22	23	24	25	26	27
28	29	30	31			

Fibulae with Pectoral. Ida ou Semlal (Morocco), late 19th to early 20th century. Silver: cast and engraved; cloisonné enamel; glass cabochons; coins. 108 × 18.5 × 8.9 cm. The Jewish Museum, New York. Purchase: Henry Herzog Family and Friends Fund in memory of Ruth Herzog, 1999-58.

Mezuzah in Case. Mumbai, India, early 1980s. Brass: cast; ink on parchment. 14.9 × 5.4 × 1.6 cm. The Jewish Museum, New York.
Gift of Erna and Samuel Daniel Divekar in memory of his parents Lt. Michael Daniel Divekar and Yerushabai Michael, 1990-160.

JULY 2024

S	M	T	W	T	F	S
	1 25 SIVAN	**2** 26 SIVAN	**3** 27 SIVAN	**4** 28 SIVAN	**5** 29 SIVAN	**6** 30 SIVAN
	Canada Day			Independence Day (US)		Rosh Hodesh Parashat Korah
7 1 TAMMUZ	**8** 2 TAMMUZ	**9** 3 TAMMUZ	**10** 4 TAMMUZ	**11** 5 TAMMUZ	**12** 6 TAMMUZ	**13** 7 TAMMUZ
Rosh Hodesh						Parashat Hukkat
14 8 TAMMUZ	**15** 9 TAMMUZ	**16** 10 TAMMUZ	**17** 11 TAMMUZ	**18** 12 TAMMUZ	**19** 13 TAMMUZ	**20** 14 TAMMUZ
						Parashat Balak
21 15 TAMMUZ	**22** 16 TAMMUZ	**23** 17 TAMMUZ	**24** 18 TAMMUZ	**25** 19 TAMMUZ	**26** 20 TAMMUZ	**27** 21 TAMMUZ
Full Moon		Fast of Tammuz				Parashat Pinehas
28 22 TAMMUZ	**29** 23 TAMMUZ	**30** 24 TAMMUZ	**31** 25 TAMMUZ			

JUNE / JULY 2024

30	Sunday	24

NOTES

1	Monday	25

Canada Day

2	Tuesday	26

3	Wednesday	27

4	Thursday	28

Independence Day (US)

5	Friday	29

6	Saturday	Rosh Hodesh Parashat Korah	30

July 2024

S	M	T	W	T	F	S
	1	2	3	4	5	6
7	8	9	10	11	12	13
14	15	16	17	18	19	20
21	22	23	24	25	26	27
28	29	30	31			

August 2024

S	M	T	W	T	F	S
				1	2	3
4	5	6	7	8	9	10
11	12	13	14	15	16	17
18	19	20	21	22	23	24
25	26	27	28	29	30	31

JULY 2024

NOTES

| 7 | Sunday | Rosh Hodesh | 1 |

| 8 | Monday | | 2 |

| 9 | Tuesday | | 3 |

| 10 | Wednesday | | 4 |

| 11 | Thursday | | 5 |

| 12 | Friday | | 6 |

| 13 | Saturday | Parashat Hukkat | 7 |

July 2024

S	M	T	W	T	F	S
	1	2	3	4	5	6
7	8	9	10	11	12	13
14	15	16	17	18	19	20
21	22	23	24	25	26	27
28	29	30	31			

August 2024

S	M	T	W	T	F	S
				1	2	3
4	5	6	7	8	9	10
11	12	13	14	15	16	17
18	19	20	21	22	23	24
25	26	27	28	29	30	31

| **14** | Sunday | 8 |

| **15** | Monday | 9 |

| **16** | Tuesday | 10 |

| **17** | Wednesday | 11 |

| **18** | Thursday | 12 |

| **19** | Friday | 13 |

| **20** | Saturday | Parashat Balak | 14 |

NOTES

July 2024

S	M	T	W	T	F	S
	1	2	3	4	5	6
7	8	9	10	11	12	13
14	15	16	17	18	19	20
21	22	23	24	25	26	27
28	29	30	31			

August 2024

S	M	T	W	T	F	S
				1	2	3
4	5	6	7	8	9	10
11	12	13	14	15	16	17
18	19	20	21	22	23	24
25	26	27	28	29	30	31

JULY 2024

NOTES

21 Sunday — 15

Full Moon

22 Monday — 16

23 Tuesday — Fast of Tammuz — 17

24 Wednesday — 18

25 Thursday — 19

July 2024

S	M	T	W	T	F	S
	1	2	3	4	5	6
7	8	9	10	11	12	13
14	15	16	17	18	19	20
21	22	23	24	25	26	27
28	29	30	31			

26 Friday — 20

August 2024

S	M	T	W	T	F	S
				1	2	3
4	5	6	7	8	9	10
11	12	13	14	15	16	17
18	19	20	21	22	23	24
25	26	27	28	29	30	31

27 Saturday — Parashat Pinehas — 21

Wall Hanging or Bed Cover. *Suzani*. Bukhara (Uzbekistan), late 19th to early 20th century.
Cotton: embroidered with silk thread; printed cotton lining; ikat silk binding. 238.8 × 152.4 cm.
The Jewish Museum, New York. Purchase: The Jewish Museum, JM 208-68a.

AUGUST 2024

S	M	T	W	T	F	S
				1 26 TAMMUZ	**2** 27 TAMMUZ	**3** 28 TAMMUZ Shabbat Mevarekhim Parashat Mattot-Masei
4 29 TAMMUZ	**5** 1 AV Rosh Hodesh	**6** 2 AV	**7** 3 AV	**8** 4 AV	**9** 5 AV	**10** 6 AV Shabbat Hazon Parashat Devarim
11 7 AV	**12** 8 AV Erev Fast of Av	**13** 9 AV Fast of Av	**14** 10 AV	**15** 11 AV	**16** 12 AV	**17** 13 AV Shabbat Nahamu Parashat Va'ethannan
18 14 AV	**19** 15 AV Full Moon	**20** 16 AV	**21** 17 AV	**22** 18 AV	**23** 19 AV	**24** 20 AV Parashat Ekev
25 21 AV	**26** 22 AV Summer Bank Holiday (UK)	**27** 23 AV	**28** 24 AV	**29** 25 AV	**30** 26 AV	**31** 27 AV Shabbat Mevarekhim Parashat Re'eh

JULY / AUGUST 2024

28 Sunday	22	

NOTES

29 Monday	23

30 Tuesday	24

31 Wednesday	25

1 Thursday	26

2 Friday	27

July 2024

S	M	T	W	T	F	S
	1	2	3	4	5	6
7	8	9	10	11	12	13
14	15	16	17	18	19	20
21	22	23	24	25	26	27
28	29	30	31			

3 Saturday	Shabbat Mevarekhim Parashat Mattot-Masei	28

August 2024

S	M	T	W	T	F	S
				1	2	3
4	5	6	7	8	9	10
11	12	13	14	15	16	17
18	19	20	21	22	23	24
25	26	27	28	29	30	31

AUGUST 2024

NOTES

4 Sunday	29
5 Monday	Rosh Hodesh 1
6 Tuesday	2
7 Wednesday	3
8 Thursday	4
9 Friday	5
10 Saturday	Shabbat Hazon Parashat Devarim 6

August 2024

S	M	T	W	T	F	S
				1	2	3
4	5	6	7	8	9	10
11	12	13	14	15	16	17
18	19	20	21	22	23	24
25	26	27	28	29	30	31

September 2024

S	M	T	W	T	F	S
1	2	3	4	5	6	7
8	9	10	11	12	13	14
15	16	17	18	19	20	21
22	23	24	25	26	27	28
29	30					

11	Sunday		7

NOTES

12	Monday	Erev Fast of Av	8

13	Tuesday	Fast of Av	9

14	Wednesday		10

15	Thursday		11

16	Friday		12

August 2024

S	M	T	W	T	F	S
				1	2	3
4	5	6	7	8	9	10
11	12	13	14	15	16	17
18	19	20	21	22	23	24
25	26	27	28	29	30	31

17	Saturday	Shabbat Nahamu	13
		Parashat Va'ethannan	

September 2024

S	M	T	W	T	F	S
1	2	3	4	5	6	7
8	9	10	11	12	13	14
15	16	17	18	19	20	21
22	23	24	25	26	27	28
29	30					

AUGUST 2024

NOTES

_____
_____
_____
_____
_____
_____
_____
_____
_____
_____
_____
_____
_____
_____
_____
_____

18 Sunday — 14

19 Monday — 15

Full Moon

20 Tuesday — 16

21 Wednesday — 17

22 Thursday — 18

23 Friday — 19

24 Saturday — Parashat Ekev — 20

August 2024

S	M	T	W	T	F	S
				1	2	3
4	5	6	7	8	9	10
11	12	13	14	15	16	17
18	19	20	21	22	23	24
25	26	27	28	29	30	31

September 2024

S	M	T	W	T	F	S
1	2	3	4	5	6	7
8	9	10	11	12	13	14
15	16	17	18	19	20	21
22	23	24	25	26	27	28
29	30					

AUGUST 2024

25 Sunday   21

26 Monday   22

Summer Bank Holiday (UK)

27 Tuesday   23

28 Wednesday   24

29 Thursday   25

30 Friday   26

31 Saturday   Shabbat Mevarekhim   27
                              Parashat Re'eh

NOTES

August 2024

S	M	T	W	T	F	S
				1	2	3
4	5	6	7	8	9	10
11	12	13	14	15	16	17
18	19	20	21	22	23	24
25	26	27	28	29	30	31

September 2024

S	M	T	W	T	F	S
1	2	3	4	5	6	7
8	9	10	11	12	13	14
15	16	17	18	19	20	21
22	23	24	25	26	27	28
29	30					

Torah Crown. Lwów, Galicia (Lviv, Ukraine), 1764/65–73. Silver: repoussé, cast, pierced, engraved, and parcel-gilt; semiprecious stones; glass.
48.6 × 30.5 × 30.5 cm. The Jewish Museum, New York. Gift of Dr. Harry G. Friedman, F 2585.

Marriage Contract. Verona (Italy), 1733. Ink and paint on parchment. 74.9 × 49.5 cm.
The Jewish Museum, New York. Gift of Isidore M. Cohen, JM 81-76.

SEPTEMBER 2024

S	M	T	W	T	F	S
1 28 AV	**2** 29 AV	**3** 30 AV	**4** 1 ELUL	**5** 2 ELUL	**6** 3 ELUL	**7** 4 ELUL
	Labor Day (US & Canada)	Rosh Hodesh	Rosh Hodesh			Parashat Shofetim
8 5 ELUL	**9** 6 ELUL	**10** 7 ELUL	**11** 8 ELUL	**12** 9 ELUL	**13** 10 ELUL	**14** 11 ELUL
						Parashat Ki Teze
15 12 ELUL	**16** 13 ELUL	**17** 14 ELUL	**18** 15 ELUL	**19** 16 ELUL	**20** 17 ELUL	**21** 18 ELUL
		Full Moon				International Day of Peace / Parashat Ki Tavo
22 19 ELUL	**23** 20 ELUL	**24** 21 ELUL	**25** 22 ELUL	**26** 23 ELUL	**27** 24 ELUL	**28** 25 ELUL
First Day of Autumn						Selihot / Parashat Nitzavim-Vayelech
29 26 ELUL	**30** 27 ELUL					
	National Day for Truth and Reconciliation (Canada)					

SEPTEMBER 2024

1   Sunday   28

2   Monday   29

Labor Day (US & Canada)

3   Tuesday   Rosh Hodesh   30

4   Wednesday   Rosh Hodesh   1

5   Thursday   2

6   Friday   3

7   Saturday   Parashat Shofetim   4

NOTES

September 2024

S	M	T	W	T	F	S
1	2	3	4	5	6	7
8	9	10	11	12	13	14
15	16	17	18	19	20	21
22	23	24	25	26	27	28
29	30					

October 2024

S	M	T	W	T	F	S
		1	2	3	4	5
6	7	8	9	10	11	12
13	14	15	16	17	18	19
20	21	22	23	24	25	26
27	28	29	30	31		

SEPTEMBER 2024

NOTES

_____
_____
_____
_____
_____
_____
_____
_____
_____
_____
_____
_____
_____
_____
_____
_____
_____
_____
_____
_____
_____
_____
_____
_____
_____

8 Sunday   5

9 Monday   6

10 Tuesday   7

11 Wednesday   8

12 Thursday   9

13 Friday   10

14 Saturday   Parashat Ki Teze 11

September 2024

S	M	T	W	T	F	S
1	2	3	4	5	6	7
8	9	10	11	12	13	14
15	16	17	18	19	20	21
22	23	24	25	26	27	28
29	30					

October 2024

S	M	T	W	T	F	S
		1	2	3	4	5
6	7	8	9	10	11	12
13	14	15	16	17	18	19
20	21	22	23	24	25	26
27	28	29	30	31		

SEPTEMBER 2024

15	Sunday	12

16	Monday	13

17	Tuesday	14

Full Moon

18	Wednesday	15

19	Thursday	16

20	Friday	17

21	Saturday	Parashat Ki Tavo	18

International Day of Peace

NOTES

September 2024

S	M	T	W	T	F	S
1	2	3	4	5	6	7
8	9	10	11	12	13	14
15	16	17	18	19	20	21
22	23	24	25	26	27	28
29	30					

October 2024

S	M	T	W	T	F	S
		1	2	3	4	5
6	7	8	9	10	11	12
13	14	15	16	17	18	19
20	21	22	23	24	25	26
27	28	29	30	31		

NOTES	**22** Sunday 19

First Day of Autumn

23 Monday   20

24 Tuesday   21

25 Wednesday   22

26 Thursday   23

September 2024

S	M	T	W	T	F	S
1	2	3	4	5	6	7
8	9	10	11	12	13	14
15	16	17	18	19	20	21
22	23	24	25	26	27	28
29	30					

27 Friday   24

October 2024

S	M	T	W	T	F	S
		1	2	3	4	5
6	7	8	9	10	11	12
13	14	15	16	17	18	19
20	21	22	23	24	25	26
27	28	29	30	31		

28 Saturday   Selihot   25
Parashat Nitzavim-Vayelech

New Year Greeting. Anton Pospischil (dates unknown), for Wiener Werkstätte, Vienna (Austria), 1903–1932. Printer: Brüder Kohn. Vienna (Austria), c. 1910–12. Lithograph on paper. 8.9 × 14 cm. The Jewish Museum, New York. Purchase: Traditional Judaica Acquisitions Committee Fund, 2006-1.

New Year Greeting. Martha Alber (1901–2000), for Wiener Werkstätte, Vienna (Austria) 1903–1932. Printer: Brüder Kohn. Vienna (Austria), c. 1910–11. Lithograph on paper. 8.9 × 14 cm. The Jewish Museum, New York. Purchase: Traditional Judaica Acquisitions Committee Fund, 2006-3.

OCTOBER 2024

S	M	T	W	T	F	S
		1 28 ELUL	**2** 29 ELUL Rosh Hashanah (Begins at Sundown) Erev Rosh Ha-Shanah	**3** 1 TISHRI Rosh Ha-Shanah 5785	**4** 2 TISHRI Rosh Ha-Shanah	**5** 3 TISHRI Shabbat Shuva Parashat Ha'Azinu
6 4 TISHRI Fast of Gedaliah	**7** 5 TISHRI	**8** 6 TISHRI	**9** 7 TISHRI	**10** 8 TISHRI	**11** 9 TISHRI Yom Kippur (Begins at Sundown) Erev Yom Kippur	**12** 10 TISHRI Yom Kippur Yizkor
13 11 TISHRI	**14** 12 TISHRI Columbus Day (US) Indigenous Peoples' Day (US) Thanksgiving Day (Canada)	**15** 13 TISHRI	**16** 14 TISHRI Erev Sukkot	**17** 15 TISHRI Full Moon First Day of Sukkot	**18** 16 TISHRI Second Day of Sukkot	**19** 17 TISHRI Hol ha-Mo-ed Sukkot
20 18 TISHRI Hol ha-Mo-ed Sukkot	**21** 19 TISHRI Hol ha-Mo-ed Sukkot	**22** 20 TISHRI Hol ha-Mo-ed Sukkot	**23** 21 TISHRI Hoshana Rabba	**24** 22 TISHRI Shemini Atzeret Yizkor	**25** 23 TISHRI Simhat Torah	**26** 24 TISHRI Shabbat Mevarekhim Parashat Bereshit
27 25 TISHRI	**28** 26 TISHRI	**29** 27 TISHRI	**30** 28 TISHRI	**31** 29 TISHRI Halloween		

SEPTEMBER / OCTOBER 2024   ELUL 5784 / TISHRI 5785

29 Sunday		26

NOTES

30 Monday		27

National Day for Truth and Reconciliation (Canada)

1 Tuesday		28

2 Wednesday	Erev Rosh Ha-Shanah	29

Rosh Hashanah (Begins at Sundown)

3 Thursday	Rosh Ha-Shanah 5785	1

4 Friday	Rosh Ha-Shanah	2

October 2024

S	M	T	W	T	F	S
		1	2	3	4	5
6	7	8	9	10	11	12
13	14	15	16	17	18	19
20	21	22	23	24	25	26
27	28	29	30	31		

5 Saturday	Shabbat Shuva / Parashat Ha'Azinu	3

November 2024

S	M	T	W	T	F	S
					1	2
3	4	5	6	7	8	9
10	11	12	13	14	15	16
17	18	19	20	21	22	23
24	25	26	27	28	29	30

Book Cover. Bezalel School. Jerusalem (Israel), c. 1924. Silver: acid etched, repoussé, granulation, and filigree; semiprecious stones. 13.2 × 9.8 × 2.9 cm. The Jewish Museum, New York. Gift of Hilde Schlesinger, 2005-6.

Torah Crown. Poland, 19th century. Silver or other metal: cast and die-stamped; glass; turquoise. 10 × 11 × 10.8 cm.
The Jewish Museum, New York. Gift of Dr. Harry G. Friedman, F 3711.

NOTES	**6** Sunday	Fast of Gedaliah	**4**

_____

_____

_____

_____

	7 Monday		**5**

_____

_____

_____

_____

	8 Tuesday		**6**

_____

_____

_____

_____

	9 Wednesday		**7**

_____

_____

_____

_____

	10 Thursday		**8**

October 2024

S	M	T	W	T	F	S
		1	2	3	4	5
6	7	8	9	10	11	12
13	14	15	16	17	18	19
20	21	22	23	24	25	26
27	28	29	30	31		

	11 Friday	Erev Yom Kippur	**9**

Yom Kippur (Begins at Sundown)

November 2024

S	M	T	W	T	F	S
					1	2
3	4	5	6	7	8	9
10	11	12	13	14	15	16
17	18	19	20	21	22	23
24	25	26	27	28	29	30

	12 Saturday	Yom Kippur Yizkor	**10**

OCTOBER 2024

13	Sunday		11

NOTES

14	Monday		12

Columbus Day (US)

Indigenous Peoples' Day (US)

Thanksgiving Day (Canada)

15	Tuesday		13

16	Wednesday	Erev Sukkot	14

17	Thursday	First Day of Sukkot	15

Full Moon

18	Friday	Second Day of Sukkot	16

October 2024

S	M	T	W	T	F	S
		1	2	3	4	5
6	7	8	9	10	11	12
13	14	15	16	17	18	19
20	21	22	23	24	25	26
27	28	29	30	31		

19	Saturday	Hol ha-Mo-ed Sukkot	17

November 2024

S	M	T	W	T	F	S
					1	2
3	4	5	6	7	8	9
10	11	12	13	14	15	16
17	18	19	20	21	22	23
24	25	26	27	28	29	30

NOTES

_____
_____
_____
_____
_____
_____
_____
_____
_____
_____
_____
_____
_____
_____
_____
_____
_____

20 Sunday   Hol ha-Mo-ed Sukkot   **18**

21 Monday   Hol ha-Mo-ed Sukkot   **19**

22 Tuesday   Hol ha-Mo-ed Sukkot   **20**

23 Wednesday   Hoshana Rabba   **21**

24 Thursday   Shemini Atzeret   **22**
                                             Yizkor

October 2024

S	M	T	W	T	F	S
		1	2	3	4	5
6	7	8	9	10	11	12
13	14	15	16	17	18	19
20	21	22	23	24	25	26
27	28	29	30	31		

25 Friday   Simhat Torah   **23**

November 2024

S	M	T	W	T	F	S
					1	2
3	4	5	6	7	8	9
10	11	12	13	14	15	16
17	18	19	20	21	22	23
24	25	26	27	28	29	30

26 Saturday   Shabbat Mevarekhim   **24**
                                  Parashat Bereshit

Torah Ark Curtain. Rahel Modigliani and three other women, dates unknown. Pitigliano (Italy), 1833/34 (date of inscription).
Net: embroidered with silk thread and silk. 251.8 × 193.7 cm. The Jewish Museum, New York.
Gift of Professor and Mrs. E. G. Machlin and Mrs. Meyer S. Siegel in honor of their father, Signor Azeglio Massimo Servi, JM 61-61.

NOVEMBER 2024

S	M	T	W	T	F	S
					1 30 TISHRI Rosh Hodesh	**2** 1 HESHVAN Rosh Hodesh Parashat No'ah
3 2 HESHVAN Daylight Saving Time Ends (US & Canada)	**4** 3 HESHVAN	**5** 4 HESHVAN Election Day (US)	**6** 5 HESHVAN	**7** 6 HESHVAN	**8** 7 HESHVAN	**9** 8 HESHVAN Parashat Lekh Lekha
10 9 HESHVAN Remembrance Sunday (UK)	**11** 10 HESHVAN Veterans Day (US) Remembrance Day (Canada & UK)	**12** 11 HESHVAN	**13** 12 HESHVAN	**14** 13 HESHVAN	**15** 14 HESHVAN Full Moon	**16** 15 HESHVAN Parashat Vayera
17 16 HESHVAN	**18** 17 HESHVAN	**19** 18 HESHVAN	**20** 19 HESHVAN	**21** 20 HESHVAN	**22** 21 HESHVAN	**23** 22 HESHVAN Parashat Hayyei Sarah
24 23 HESHVAN	**25** 24 HESHVAN	**26** 25 HESHVAN	**27** 26 HESHVAN	**28** 27 HESHVAN Thanksgiving Day (US)	**29** 28 HESHVAN	**30** 29 HESHVAN Shabbat Mevarekhim Parashat Toledot

OCTOBER / NOVEMBER 2024 TISHRI / HESHVAN 5785

תשרי / חשון

27 Sunday		25
28 Monday		26
29 Tuesday		27
30 Wednesday		28
31 Thursday		29

NOTES

Halloween

1 Friday	Rosh Hodesh	30
2 Saturday	Rosh Hodesh Parashat No'ah	1

October 2024

S	M	T	W	T	F	S
		1	2	3	4	5
6	7	8	9	10	11	12
13	14	15	16	17	18	19
20	21	22	23	24	25	26
27	28	29	30	31		

November 2024

S	M	T	W	T	F	S
					1	2
3	4	5	6	7	8	9
10	11	12	13	14	15	16
17	18	19	20	21	22	23
24	25	26	27	28	29	30

NOVEMBER 2024

NOTES

3 Sunday   2

Daylight Saving Time Ends
(US & Canada)

4 Monday   3

5 Tuesday   4

Election Day (US)

6 Wednesday   5

7 Thursday   6

8 Friday   7

9 Saturday   Parashat Lekh Lekha   8

November 2024

S	M	T	W	T	F	S
					1	2
3	4	5	6	7	8	9
10	11	12	13	14	15	16
17	18	19	20	21	22	23
24	25	26	27	28	29	30

December 2024

S	M	T	W	T	F	S
1	2	3	4	5	6	7
8	9	10	11	12	13	14
15	16	17	18	19	20	21
22	23	24	25	26	27	28
29	30	31				

Torah Finials. August Ferdinand Gentzmer (1758/59–1808; active from 1789). Berlin (Germany), 1789-1802.
Silver: repoussé, pierced, cast, engraved, and parcel-gilt. Each: 52.7 × 12 cm. The Jewish Museum, New York.
Gift of the Danzig Jewish Community, D 173a-b.

NOTES

_____

_____

_____

_____

_____

_____

_____

_____

_____

_____

_____

_____

_____

_____

_____

_____

_____

10 Sunday   9

Remembrance Sunday (UK)

11 Monday   10

Veterans Day (US)
Remembrance Day (Canada & UK)

12 Tuesday   11

13 Wednesday   12

14 Thursday   13

November 2024

S	M	T	W	T	F	S
					1	2
3	4	5	6	7	8	9
10	11	12	13	14	15	16
17	18	19	20	21	22	23
24	25	26	27	28	29	30

December 2024

S	M	T	W	T	F	S
1	2	3	4	5	6	7
8	9	10	11	12	13	14
15	16	17	18	19	20	21
22	23	24	25	26	27	28
29	30	31				

15 Friday   14

Full Moon

16 Saturday   *Parashat Vayera*   15

NOVEMBER 2024

| 17 | Sunday | 16 |

NOTES

| 18 | Monday | 17 |

| 19 | Tuesday | 18 |

| 20 | Wednesday | 19 |

| 21 | Thursday | 20 |

| 22 | Friday | 21 |

November 2024

S	M	T	W	T	F	S
					1	2
3	4	5	6	7	8	9
10	11	12	13	14	15	16
17	18	19	20	21	22	23
24	25	26	27	28	29	30

| 23 | Saturday | Parashat Hayyei Sarah | 22 |

December 2024

S	M	T	W	T	F	S
1	2	3	4	5	6	7
8	9	10	11	12	13	14
15	16	17	18	19	20	21
22	23	24	25	26	27	28
29	30	31				

NOTES

_____
_____
_____
_____
_____
_____
_____
_____
_____
_____
_____
_____
_____
_____
_____
_____
_____
_____
_____

24 Sunday — 23

25 Monday — 24

26 Tuesday — 25

27 Wednesday — 26

28 Thursday — 27

November 2024

S	M	T	W	T	F	S
					1	2
3	4	5	6	7	8	9
10	11	12	13	14	15	16
17	18	19	20	21	22	23
24	25	26	27	28	29	30

December 2024

S	M	T	W	T	F	S
1	2	3	4	5	6	7
8	9	10	11	12	13	14
15	16	17	18	19	20	21
22	23	24	25	26	27	28
29	30	31				

Thanksgiving Day (US)

29 Friday — 28

30 Saturday — 29
Shabbat Mevarekhim
Parashat Toledot

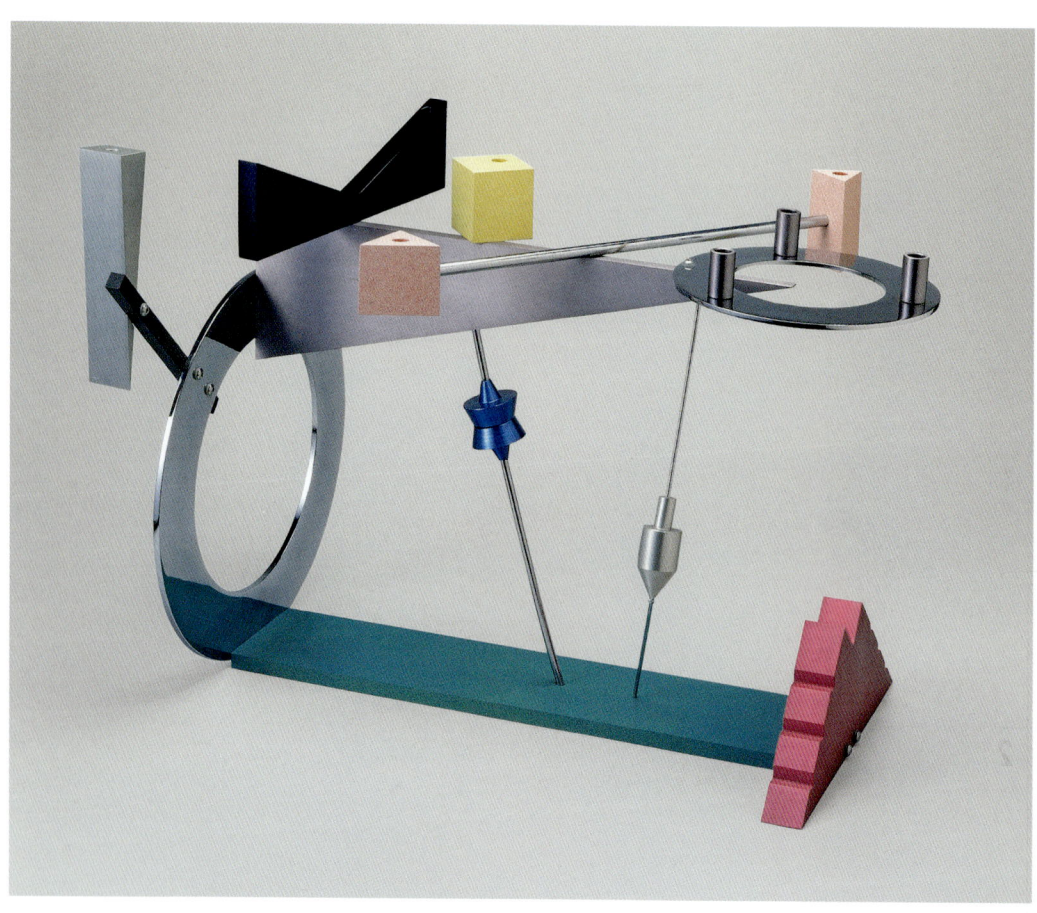

Hanukkah Lamp. *Menorah #7*. Peter Shire (American, b. 1947). Los Angeles, California, United States, 1986. Steel: painted; aluminum: anodized; chromium. 54 × 57.2 × 43.2 cm. The Jewish Museum, New York. Purchase: Judaica Acquisitions Endowment Fund, 1989-20.

DECEMBER 2024

S	M	T	W	T	F	S
1 30 HESHVAN Rosh Hodesh	**2** 1 KISLEV Rosh Hodesh	**3** 2 KISLEV	**4** 3 KISLEV	**5** 4 KISLEV	**6** 5 KISLEV	**7** 6 KISLEV Parashat Vayeze
8 7 KISLEV	**9** 8 KISLEV	**10** 9 KISLEV Human Rights Day	**11** 10 KISLEV	**12** 11 KISLEV	**13** 12 KISLEV	**14** 13 KISLEV Parashat Vayishlah
15 14 KISLEV Full Moon	**16** 15 KISLEV	**17** 16 KISLEV	**18** 17 KISLEV	**19** 18 KISLEV	**20** 19 KISLEV	**21** 20 KISLEV First Day of Winter Parashat Vayeshev
22 21 KISLEV	**23** 22 KISLEV	**24** 23 KISLEV	**25** 24 KISLEV Christmas Hanukkah (Begins at Sundown) Erev Hanukkah	**26** 25 KISLEV Kwanzaa Begins Boxing Day (Canada & UK) First Day of Hanukkah	**27** 26 KISLEV Second Day of Hanukkah	**28** 27 KISLEV Shabbat Mevarekhim Parashat Mi-kez Third Day of Hanukkah
29 28 KISLEV Fourth Day of Hanukkah	**30** 29 KISLEV Fifth Day of Hanukkah	**31** 30 KISLEV Rosh Hodesh Sixth Day of Hanukkah				

DECEMBER 2024

1   Sunday   Rosh Hodesh   30

NOTES

2   Monday   Rosh Hodesh   1

3   Tuesday   2

4   Wednesday   3

5   Thursday   4

6   Friday   5

December 2024

S	M	T	W	T	F	S
1	2	3	4	5	6	7
8	9	10	11	12	13	14
15	16	17	18	19	20	21
22	23	24	25	26	27	28
29	30	31				

7   Saturday   Parashat Vayeze   6

January 2025

S	M	T	W	T	F	S
			1	2	3	4
5	6	7	8	9	10	11
12	13	14	15	16	17	18
19	20	21	22	23	24	25
26	27	28	29	30	31	

DECEMBER 2024

NOTES

_____
_____
_____
_____
_____
_____
_____
_____
_____
_____
_____
_____
_____
_____
_____
_____
_____
_____
_____
_____

8 Sunday 7

9 Monday 8

10 Tuesday 9

Human Rights Day

11 Wednesday 10

12 Thursday 11

13 Friday 12

14 Saturday Parashat Vayishlah 13

December 2024

S	M	T	W	T	F	S
1	2	3	4	5	6	7
8	9	10	11	12	13	14
15	16	17	18	19	20	21
22	23	24	25	26	27	28
29	30	31				

January 2025

S	M	T	W	T	F	S
			1	2	3	4
5	6	7	8	9	10	11
12	13	14	15	16	17	18
19	20	21	22	23	24	25
26	27	28	29	30	31	

DECEMBER 2024

15 Sunday		14

Full Moon

16 Monday		15

17 Tuesday		16

18 Wednesday		17

19 Thursday		18

20 Friday		19

21 Saturday	Parashat Vayeshev	20

First Day of Winter

NOTES

December 2024

S	M	T	W	T	F	S
1	2	3	4	5	6	7
8	9	10	11	12	13	14
15	16	17	18	19	20	21
22	23	24	25	26	27	28
29	30	31				

January 2025

S	M	T	W	T	F	S
			1	2	3	4
5	6	7	8	9	10	11
12	13	14	15	16	17	18
19	20	21	22	23	24	25
26	27	28	29	30	31	

Multipurpose Cube. Zelig Segal (Israeli, 1933–2015). Israel, 1986. Aluminum: milled. 10 × 10 × 10 cm.
The Jewish Museum, New York. Gift of Marcia Riklis,1999-6.

DECEMBER 2024

22 Sunday   21

NOTES

23 Monday   22

24 Tuesday   23

25 Wednesday   Erev Hanukkah   24

Christmas
Hanukkah (Begins at Sundown)

26 Thursday   First Day of Hanukkah   25

Kwanzaa Begins
Boxing Day (Canada & UK)

27 Friday   Second Day of Hanukkah   26

28 Saturday   Shabbat Mevarekhim   27
    Parashat Mi-kez
    Third Day of Hanukkah

December 2024

S	M	T	W	T	F	S
1	2	3	4	5	6	7
8	9	10	11	12	13	14
15	16	17	18	19	20	21
22	23	24	25	26	27	28
29	30	31				

January 2025

S	M	T	W	T	F	S
			1	2	3	4
5	6	7	8	9	10	11
12	13	14	15	16	17	18
19	20	21	22	23	24	25
26	27	28	29	30	31	

DECEMBER 2024 / JANUARY 2025

NOTES

29	Sunday	Fourth Day of Hanukkah 28

_____

_____

_____

_____

30	Monday	Fifth Day of Hanukkah 29

_____

_____

_____

31	Tuesday	Rosh Hodesh 30
		Sixth Day of Hanukkah

_____

_____

_____

1	Wednesday	Seventh Day of Hanukkah 1

_____

New Year's Day

2	Thursday	Eighth Day of Hanukkah 2

December 2024

S	M	T	W	T	F	S
1	2	3	4	5	6	7
8	9	10	11	12	13	14
15	16	17	18	19	20	21
22	23	24	25	26	27	28
29	30	31				

3	Friday	3

January 2025

S	M	T	W	T	F	S
			1	2	3	4
5	6	7	8	9	10	11
12	13	14	15	16	17	18
19	20	21	22	23	24	25
26	27	28	29	30	31	

4	Saturday	4

TORAH AND PROPHETIC READINGS

Date	Torah Readings	Prophetic Readings	Sephardic Prophetic Readings
2023			
Sept. 2	Deut. 26:1-29:8	Isaiah 60:1-22	
Sept. 9	Deut. 29:9-31:30	Isaiah 61:10-63:9	
Sept. 16	Gen. 21:1-34; Num. 29:1-6	I Samuel 1:1-2:10	
Sept. 17	Gen. 22:1-24; Num. 29:1-6	Jerem. 31:1-19	
Sept. 18	Ex. 32:11-14, 34:1 10	(afternoon) Isaiah 55:6-56:8	
Sept. 23	Deut. 32:1-52	Hosea 14:2-10; Micah 7:18-20; Joel 2:15-27	
Sept. 25	(morning) Lev. 16:1-34; Num. 29:7-11	Isaiah 57:14-58:14	
	(afternoon) Lev. 18:1-30	Jonah 1:1-4:11; Micah 7:18-20	
Sept. 30	Lev. 22:26-23:44; Num. 29:12-16	Zech. 14:1-21	
Oct. 1	Lev. 22:26-23:44; Num. 29:12-16	I Kings 8:2-21	
Oct. 2	Num. 29:17-25		
Oct. 3	Num. 29:20-28		
Oct. 4	Num. 29:23-31		
Oct. 5	Num. 29:26-34		
Oct. 6	Num. 29:26-34		
Oct. 7	Deut. 14:22-16:17; Num. 29:35-30:1	I Kings 8:54-9:1	I Kings 8:54–66
Oct. 8	Deut. 33:1-34:12; Gen. 1:1-2:3; Num. 29:35-30:1	Joshua 1:1-18	
Oct. 14	Gen. 1:1-6:8	I Samuel 20:18-42	
Oct. 15	Num. 28:1-15		
Oct. 16	Num. 28:1-15		
Oct. 21	Gen. 6:9-11:32	Isaiah 54:1-55:5	Isaiah 54:1–10
Oct. 28	Gen. 12:1-17:27	Isaiah 40:27-41:16	
Nov. 4	Gen. 18:1-22:24	II Kings 4:1-37	II Kings 4:1–23
Nov. 11	Gen. 23:1-25:18	I Kings 1:1-31	
Nov. 14	Num. 28:1-15		
Nov. 18	Gen. 25:19-28:9	Mal. 1:1-2:7	
Nov. 25	Gen. 28:10-32:2	Hosea 12:13-14:10	Hosea 11:7–12:12
Dec. 2	Gen. 32:3-36:43	Obadiah 1:1-21	
Dec. 8	Num. 7:1-17		
Dec. 9	Gen. 37:1-40:23; Num. 7:18-23	Zech. 2:14-4:7	
Dec. 10	Num. 7:24-35		
Dec. 11	Num. 7:30-41		
Dec. 12	Num. 7:36-47		
Dec. 13	Num. 28:1-15, 7:42-47		
Dec. 14	Num. 7:48-59		
Dec. 15	Num. 7:54-8:4		
Dec. 16	Gen. 41:1-44:17	I Kings 3:15-4:1	
Dec. 22	Ex. 32:11-14, 34:1-10	(afternoon) Isaiah 55:6-56:8	
Dec. 23	Gen. 44:18-47:27	Ezek. 37:15-28	
Dec. 30	Gen. 47:28-50:26	I Kings 2:1-12	
2024			
Jan. 6	Ex. 1:1-6:1	Isaiah 27:6-28:13, 29:22-23	Jerem. 1:1-2:3
Jan. 7	Num. 28:1-15		
Jan. 13	Ex. 6:2-9:35	Ezek. 28:25-29:21	
Jan. 20	Ex. 10:1-13:16	Jerem. 46:13-28	
Jan. 27	Ex. 13:17-17:16	Judges 4:4-5:31	Judges 5:1-31
Feb. 3	Ex. 18:1-20:23	Isaiah 6:1-7:6, 9:5-6	Isaiah 6:1-13
Feb. 9	Num. 28:1-15		
Feb. 10	Ex. 21:1-24:18; Num. 28:9-15	Isaiah 66:1-24	
Feb. 17	Ex. 25:1-27:19	I Kings 5:26-6:13	
Feb. 24	Ex. 27:20-30:10	Ezek. 43:10-27	
Mar. 2	Ex. 30:11-34:35	I Kings 18:1-39	I Kings 18:20-39
Mar. 9	Ex. 35:1-38:20, 30:11-16	II Kings 12:1-17	I Kings 7:13-26; II Kings 11:17-12:17
Mar. 10	Num. 28:1-15		
Mar. 11	Num. 28:1-15		
Mar. 16	Ex. 38:21-40:38	I Kings 7:51-8:21	I Kings 7:40-50
Mar. 21	Ex. 32:11-14, 34:1-10	(afternoon) Isaiah 55:6-56:8	
Mar. 23	Lev. 1:1-5:26; Deut. 25:17-19	I Samuel 15:2-34	I Samuel 15:1-34
Mar. 24	Ex. 17:8-16		
Mar. 30	Lev. 6:1-8:36; Num. 19:1-22	Ezek. 36:16-38	Ezek. 36:16-36
Apr. 6	Lev. 9:1-11:47; Ex. 12:1-20	Ezek. 45:16-46:18	Ezek. 45:18-46:15
Apr. 9	Num. 28:1-15		
Apr. 13	Lev. 12:1-13:59	II Kings 4:42-5:19	
Apr. 20	Lev. 14:1-15:33	Malachi 3:4-24	
Apr. 23	Ex. 12:21-51; Num. 28:16-25	Joshua 5:2-6:1	
Apr. 24	Lev. 22:26-23:44; Num. 28:16-25	II Kings 23:1-9, 23:21-25	

Date	Torah Readings	Prophetic Readings	Sephardic Prophetic Readings
Apr. 25	Ex. 13:1-16; Num. 28:19-25		
Apr. 26	Ex. 22:24-23:19; Num. 28:19-25		
Apr. 27	Ex. 33:12-34:26; Num. 28:19-25	Ezek. 37:1-14	
Apr. 28	Ex. 34:1-26; Num. 9:1-14; 28:19-25		
Apr. 29	Ex. 13:17-15:26; Num. 28:19-25	II Samuel 22:1-51	
Apr. 30	Deut. 15:19-16:17; Num. 28:19-25	Isaiah 10:32-12:6	
May 4	Lev. 16:1-18:30	Amos 9:7-15	
May 8	Num. 28:1-15		
May 9	Num. 28:1-15		
May 11	Lev. 19:1-20:27	Ezek. 22:1-19	Ezek. 20:2-20
May 18	Lev. 21:1-24:23	Ezek. 44:15-31	
May 25	Lev. 25:1-26:2	Jerem. 32:6-27	
June 1	Lev. 26:3-27:34	Jerem. 16:19-17:14	
June 7	Num. 28:1-15		
June 8	Num. 1:1-4:20	Hosea 2:1-22	
June 12	Ex. 19:1-20:23; Num. 28:26-31	Ezek. 1:1-28, 3:12	
June 13	Deut. 15:19-16:17; Num. 28:26-31	Habakkuk 2:20-3:19	
June 15	Num. 4:21-7:89	Judges 13:2-25	
June 22	Num. 8:1-12:16	Zech. 2:14-4:7	
June 29	Num. 13:1-15:41	Joshua 2:1-24	
July 6	Num. 16:1-18:32, 28:9-15	Isaiah 66:1-24; I Samuel 20:18,42	
July 7	Num. 28:1-15		
July 13	Num. 19:1-22:1	Judges 11:1-33	
July 20	Num. 22:2-25:9	Micah 5:6-6:8	
July 23	Ex. 32:11-14, 34:1-10	(afternoon) Isaiah 55:6-56:8	
July 27	Num. 25:10-30:1	Jerem. 1:1-2:3	
Aug. 3	Num. 30:2-36:13	Jerem. 2:4-28, 3:4	
Aug. 5	Num. 28:1-15		
Aug. 10	Deut. 1:1-3:22	Isaiah 1:1-27	
Aug. 13	(morning) Deut. 4:25-40	(morning) Jerem. 8:13-9:23	
	(afternoon) Ex. 32:11-14; 34:1-10	(afternoon) Isaiah 55:6-56:8	
Aug. 17	Deut. 3:23-7:11	Isaiah 40:1-26	
Aug. 24	Deut. 7:12-11:25	Isaiah 49:14-51:3	
Aug. 31	Deut. 11:26-16:17	Isaiah 54:11-55:5	
Sept. 3	Num. 28:1-15		
Sept. 4	Num. 28:1-15		
Sept. 7	Deut. 16:18-21:9	Isaiah 51:12-52:12	
Sept. 14	Deut. 21:10-25:19	Isaiah 54:1-10	
Sept. 21	Deut. 26:1-29:8	Isaiah 60:1-22	
Sept. 28	Deut. 29:9-31:30	Isaiah 61:10-63:9	
Oct. 3	Gen. 21:1-34; Num. 29:1-6	I Samuel 1:1-2:10	
Oct. 4	Gen. 22:1-24; Num. 29:1-6	Jerem. 31:1-19	
Oct. 5	Deut. 32:1-52	Hosea 14:2-10; Micah 7:18-20; Joel 2:15-27	
Oct. 6	Ex. 32:11-14, 34:1-10	(afternoon) Isaiah 55:6-56:8	
Oct. 12	(morning) Lev. 16:1-34; Num. 29:7-11	(morning) Isaiah 57:14-58:14	
	(afternoon) Lev. 18:1-30	(afternoon) Jonah 1:1-4:11; Micah 7:18-20	
Oct. 17	Lev. 22:26-23:44; Num. 29:12-16	Zech. 14:1-21	
Oct. 18	Lev. 22:26-23:44; Num. 29:12-16	I Kings 8:2-21	
Oct. 19	Ex. 33:12-34:26; Num. 29:17-22	Ezek. 38:18-39:16	
Oct. 20	Num. 29:20-28, 29:20-25		
Oct. 21	Num. 29:23-31, 29:23-28		
Oct. 22	Num. 29:26-34, 29:26-31		
Oct. 23	Num. 29:26-34, 29:29-34		
Oct. 24	Deut. 14:22-16:17; Num. 29:35-30:1	I Kings 8:54-9:1	I Kings 8:54-66
Oct. 25	Deut. 33:1-34:12; Gen. 1:1-2:3; Num. 29:35-30:1	Joshua 1:1-18	
Oct. 26	Gen. 1:1-6:8	Isaiah 42:5-43:10	Isaiah 42:5-21
Nov. 1	Num. 28:1-15		
Nov. 2	Gen. 6:9-11:32; Num. 28:9-15	Isaiah 66:1-24	
Nov. 9	Gen. 12:1-17:27	Isaiah 40:27-41:16	
Nov. 16	Gen. 18:1-22:24	II Kings 4:1-37	II Kings 4:1-23
Nov. 23	Gen. 23:1-25:18	I Kings 1:1-31	
Nov. 30	Gen. 25:19-28:9	I Samuel 20:18-42	
Dec. 1	Num. 28:1-15		
Dec. 2	Num. 28:1-15		
Dec. 7	Gen. 28:10-32:3	Hosea 12:13-14:10	Hosea 11:7-12:12
Dec. 14	Gen. 32:4-36:43	Obadiah 1:1-21	
Dec. 21	Gen. 37:1-40:23	Amos 2:6-3:8	
Dec. 26	Num. 7:1-17		
Dec. 27	Num. 7:18-29		
Dec. 28	Gen. 41:1-44:17; Num. 7:24-29	Zech. 2:14-4:7	
Dec. 29	Num. 7:30-41		
Dec. 30	Num. 7:36-47		
Dec. 31	Num. 28:1-15, 7:42-47		

JEWISH HOLIDAYS

	Hebrew Date	Candle Blessings	Torah Readings	Prophetic Readings	Additional Readings
ROSH HA-SHANAH (The New Year)	Tishri 1 & 2 First day can fall only on Monday, Tuesday, Thursday, Saturday	1,2	First day: Gen. 21:1–34; Num. 29:1-6 Second day: Gen. 22:1–24; Num. 29:1–6	First day: I Samuel 1:1–2:10 Second day: Jeremiah 31:1–19	Mahzor (special prayer book) for Rosh Hashanah
TZOM GEDALIAH (Fast of Gedaliah)	Tishri 3 Adar 13		Ex. 32:11–14; 34:1–10	Afternoon: Isaiah 55:6–56:8	‡ "Answer us, O Lord, answer us."
YOM KIPPUR (Day of Atonement)	Tishri 10 Can fall only on Monday, Wednesday, Thursday, Saturday	1a,2	Morning: Lev. 16:1–34; Num. 29:7–11 Afternoon: Lev. 18:1–30	Morning: Isaiah 57:14–58:14 Afternoon: Jonah 1–4; Micah 7:18–20	Mahzor for Yom Kippur; Yizkor (memorial prayers)
SUKKOT (Tabernacles)	Tishri 15–21 Can fall only on Monday, Tuesday, Thursday, Saturday	1,2	Lev. 22:26–23:44; Num. 29:12–16	First day: Zechariah 14:1–21 Second day: I Kings 8:2–21	Full Hallel on all days § "... May there come before you ..." Book of Ecclesiastes Lulav and etrog Kohelet ★★★
SHEMINI ATZERET (The Eighth Day's Assembly)	Tishri 22 Can fall only on Monday, Tuesday, Thursday, Saturday	1,2	Deut. 15:19–16:17; Num. 29:35–30:1	I Kings 8:54–9:1	Hallel Prayer for rain "... May there come before you ..." Yizkor
SIMHAT TORAH (Rejoicing of the Torah)	Tishri 23 Can fall only on Sunday, Tuesday, Wednesday, Friday	1,2	Deut. 33:1–34:12; Gen. 1:1–2:3; Num. 29:35–30:1	Joshua 1:1–18	Hallel § "... May there come before you ..."
HANUKKAH	Kislev 25–Tevet 3	3,4,2#	See note†	First Shabbat: Zechariah 2:14–4:7 Second Shabbat (when there is one): I Kings 7:40–50	Full Hallel on all days ‖ "... On the miracles ..."
FAST OF THE 10TH OF THE MONTH OF TEVET	Tevet 10		Ex. 32:11–14; 34:1–10	Afternoon: Isaiah 55:6–56:8	‡ "Answer us, O Lord, answer us ..."
TU B'SHEVAT (New Year for the Trees)	Shevat 15				
TA'ANIT ESTHER (Fast of Esther)	Day before Purim		Ex. 32:11–14; 34:1–10	Afternoon: Isaiah 55:6–56:8	‡ "Answer us, O Lord, answer us ..."

Theme or Element	Biblical / Historial Significance	Seasonal Significance	Mood / Setting	Selected Customs
Creation World is judged regarding people "On Rosh Hashanah it is written . . ." "Today is the birthday of the world"	"And in the seventh month, on the first day of the month, you shall have a holy convocation . . ." —Num. 29:1–6	Beginning of end of productive year	Putting behind to start anew Community Steady high	Dipping apples in honey Sending wishes for a good and a sweet year Casting crumbs (sin) into the river Blowing shofar Round hallah
Divine displeasure	Assassination of Gedaliah, governor of Judah, who had been appointed by Nebuchadnezzar, 586 B.C.		Human supplication for mercy Mild low	Fasting from morning to evening
Humanity is judged Prayer/charity/repentance "And on Yom Kippur it is sealed . . ."	"And on the tenth day of this seventh month you shall have a holy convocation; and you shall afflict your souls: You shall do no manner of work . . ." —Num. 29:7–11		Introspection Returning self before God Heavy high	Charity Fasting and abstinence Wearing white garments
Redemption Sukkat Shalom (Tabernacle of Peace) Hospitality Foretaste of messianic harmony	Israelites wandering through the desert "And on the fifteenth day of the seventh month you shall have a holy convocation . . ." —Num. 29:12–34	Final harvest festival Preparation for winter hibernation	Brotherhood/sister-hood/peoplehood Joy	Eating (sleeping) in the sukkah Inviting guests Waving the lulav and etrog
World is judged regarding the availability of water	"On the eighth day you shall have a solemn assembly . . ." —Num. 29:35–39	Apprehension concerning there being a good rainy season to prepare the land for the next growing period	Collective concern Low	
Torah is cosmic teaching Circularity (never-ending circle of Torah and of the Jewish year)			Wedding ceremony "Happy are we! How goodly is our portion, how pleasant our lot, how beautiful our heritage . . ." Ecstasy	Dancing with the Torah Children carrying flags and apples Getting high (drunk) on Torah
Spreading light	Defeat of Syrians by Macca-bees; cleansing of the Temple; rededicating the people to Judaism, 167 B.C.	Winter solstice Midwinter fire festival	Emergence from darkness to light Light high	Lighting candles Playing dreidel Eating potato latkes
Divine displeasure	Commencement of siege of Jerusalem by Nebuchadnezzar, 586 B.C.		Human supplication for mercy Mild low	Fasting from morning to evening
Reawakening of nature Reestablishing the divine flow	Date from which to count the years of the tree for purposes of tithe Dedication of first fruits Personal use of the fruits	First signs of spring Sap begins rising in trees in Israel	Good fruits Rich soil Sensuous high	Planting trees Eating varieties of nuts and fruits, especially carob
Supplication	Jews of Persia praying for overturning of Haman's plot to destroy them			Fasting from morning to evening

	Hebrew Date	Candle Blessings	Torah Readings	Prophetic Readings	Additional Readings
PURIM (Feast of Lots)	Adar 14		Ex. 17:8–16		Book of Esther | | "... On the miracles ..."
PESAH (Passover)	Nisan 15–22 First day can fall only on Sunday, Tuesday, Thursday, Saturday	1,2★★	First day: Ex. 12:21–51; Num. 28:16–25 Second day: Lev. 22:26–23:44; Num. 28:16–25 Seventh day: Ex. 13:17–15:26; Num. 28:19–25 Eighth day: Deut. 15:19–16:17; Num. 28:19–25*	First day: Joshua 3:5–7; 5:2–6:1 Second day: II Kings 23:1–9, 21–25 Seventh day: II Samuel 22:1–51 Eighth day: Isaiah 10:32–12:6	Full Hallel first two days Partial Hallel last six days § "... May there come before you ..." Song of Songs Yizkor last day
OMER (Counting of the Omer)	Nisan 16– Sivan 5				
YOM HA-SHOAH (Day of Remembrance of the Holocaust)	Nisan 27				
YOM HA-ATZMA'UT (Israel Independence Day)	Iyar 5				Hallel
LAG B'OMER (33rd Day in Omer Count)	Iyar 18				
SHAVUOT (Feast of Weeks)	Sivan 6–7 First day can fall only on Sunday, Monday, Wednesday, Friday	1,2	First day: Ex. 19:1–20:23; Num. 28:26–31 Second day: Deut. 15:19–16:17★; Num. 28: 26–31	First day: Ezekiel 1:1–28, 3:12 Second day: Habakkuk 2:20–3:19	Full Hallel § "... May there come before you ..." Book of Ruth Yizkor second day
FAST OF THE 17TH OF THE MONTH OF TAMMUZ	Tammuz 17		Ex. 32:11–14, 34:1–10	Afternoon: Isaiah 55:6–56:8	‡ "Answer us, O Lord, answer us ..."
TISHA B'AV	Av 9		Deut. 4:25–40 Afternoon: Ex. 32:11–14, 34:1–10	Morning: Jeremiah 8:13–9:23 Isaiah 55:6–56:8	Book of Lamentations
ROSH HODESH (The New Moon)			Num. 28:1–15		Partial Hallel § "... May there come before you ..."

★ If the last day of Pesah or the second day of Shavuot falls on Shabbat, there is a special Torah reading: Deut. 14:22–16:17.

† On Hanukkah, essentially what is read is Num. 7:1–8:4, a description of the offerings made by the princes of the twelve tribes at the time the Tabernacle was dedicated in the desert. This serves as the paradigm for the rededication celebration of Hanukkah. The basic order is Day 1, Num 7:1–17; Day 2, Num 7:18–29; Day 3, Num. 7:24–35; Day 4, Num. 7:30–41; Day 5, Num. 7:36–47; Day 6, Num. 7:42–53; Day 7, Num. 7:48–59; Day 8, Num. 7:54–84. Because the New Moon (either one or two days) occurs during the holiday, as does either one Shabbat or two Shabbatot, and because the New Moon and Shabbat can coincide, it is too difficult to list all the Torah readings for all eventualities. Consequently, one must check each year for the correct Torah readings for Hanukkah for that year.

‡ "Answer us, O Lord, answer us ..." (Anenu) is a special prayer added to the Amidah (standing devotion) on fast days entreating God to deliver us from our troubles.

§ "... May there come before you ..." (Ya'aleh v'Yavo)—a prayer added to the Amidah and Birkat Hamazon (grace after meals) on festivals and New Moons—petitions God to remember the whole House of Israel for good and blessing so that our festivals may be celebrated in joy.

Theme or Element	Biblical / Historial Significance	Seasonal Significance	Mood / Setting	Selected Customs
Giving gifts Giving charity Overcoming duality	Victory of Jews over Haman through the intercession of Esther and Mordecai	Spring rites festival	Breaking of inhibitions, getting so drunk as not to distinguish between "Blessed Mordecai and cursed Haman" Dionysian high	Blotting out Haman's name with graggers Sending gifts of food to friends Giving to the poor
Creation/Revelation World is judged regarding produce Freedom Birth—breaking out	Redemption of Israelites from Egyptian slavery "And in the first month, on the fourteenth day of the month, is the Lord's Passover . . ." —Num. 28:16–25	New Year festival: first month of year First crops (barley) First calvings	Family Reflective Liberation through discipline Serious high	Removing hametz (leaven) Eating matzah Participating in a seder
Growth Counting Anticipating	"And you shall count unto you from the morrow after the day of rest . . . seven weeks . . ." Plague on disciples of R. Akiba, 2nd century	Apprehension concerning fate of latter crops—will the seed take? Lev. 23:15–16	Semi-mourning Expectant, sober Anticipation	Counting the days
God is judged	The destruction of six million Jews during World War II while the world, God, and man remained silent		Reflective Somber	
Strength	Declaration of an independent state of Israel in 1948		Secular joy	Parades
Release from mourning Spring festival	The plague of R. Akiba's disciples lifted	Spring outing	Springtime Fantasy, fancy, and frolic	Picnics
Revelation World is judged regarding fruits Maturity Receiving	Giving of the Torah to Israelites at Mt. Sinai "When you bring a new meal offering unto the Lord in your feast of weeks, you shall have a holy convocation . . ." —Num. 28:28–31	First reapings of fruits and produce	Community Openness, sharing, receptivity Climactic high	Staying up all night studying Torah Spreading grasses in synagogue Dairy products
Divine displeasure	Moses breaks the first tablets First breach in Jerusalem's walls by Nebuchadnezzar's forces		Human supplication for mercy Mild low	Fasting from morning to evening
Contemplating the ashes upon which the new world will rise Mourning	Destruction of the First and Second Temples—586 B.C. and 70 A.D.		Somber mourning Heavy	Fasting Sitting on the floor Singing dirges
Renewal		Reemergence of the moon after its three-day withdrawal	Semi-holiday for women Light	

|| ". . . on the miracles . . ." (Al Hanisim) is a prayer added to the Amidah and Birkat Hamazon during Hanukkah and Purim, thanking God for the miracles he performed for our ancestors and for us.
Candle blessings:
1. Blessed are You, Adonai our God, Ruler of the Universe, who has sanctified us with His commandments and commanded us to light the [Shabbat and] Festival light.
1a. Blessed are You, Adonai our God, Ruler of the Universe, who has sanctified us with His commandments and commanded us to light the Yom Kippur light.
2. Blessed are You, Adonai our God, Ruler of the Universe, who has given us life and preserved us and enabled us to reach this season.
3. Blessed are You, Adonai our God, Ruler of the Universe, who has sanctified us with His commandments and commanded us to light the Hanukkah lights.
4. Blessed are You, Adonai our God, Ruler of the Universe, who has done great miracles for our ancestors, in those days, at this time.
First night of Hanukkah only.
★★ On the last two nights of Pesah, only the first blessing is said.
★★★ When Shemini Atzeret falls on Shabbat, Kohelet is read then.

SHABBAT AND HOLIDAY CANDLE-LIGHTING TIMES
FOR SEPTEMBER 2023 THROUGH DECEMBER 2024

Times are adjusted for Daylight Saving Time. In Jerusalem, candle-lighting times shown are 40 minutes before sundown.
In the diaspora, times shown are 18 minutes before sundown.

	JERUSALEM GMT	LONDON EST	N.Y.C. EST	PHILA. EST	WASH., D.C. EST	MIAMI EST	DETROIT EST	TORONTO EST	HOUSTON CST	CHICAGO CST	L.A. PST
2023											
Sept. 1	6:23	7:29	7:10	7:14	7:20	7:22	7:48	7:35	7:25	7:06	7:00
Sept. 8	6:14	7:13	6:58	7:03	7:09	7:14	7:36	7:23	7:17	6:54	6:51
Sept. 15	6:05	6:57	6:47	6:51	6:58	7:07	7:24	7:10	7:08	6:42	6:41
Sept. 16	7:21	8:04	7:44	7:48	7:55	7:58	8:22	8:09	8:01	7:40	7:35
Sept. 22	5:56	6:41	6:35	6:40	6:47	6:59	7:11	6:57	7:00	6:30	6:31
Sept. 24	5:53	6:37	6:31	6:36	6:44	6:57	7:08	6:53	6:57	6:26	6:29
Sept. 29	5:47	6:25	6:23	6:28	6:36	6:51	6:59	6:44	6:51	6:17	6:22
Sept. 30		7:31	7:20	7:25	7:32	7:43	7:57	7:43	7:44	7:15	7:16
Oct. 6	5:38	6:09	6:11	6:17	6:25	6:44	6:47	6:32	6:43	6:06	6:12
Oct. 7		7:15	7:09	7:14	7:21	7:35	7:45	7:31	7:35	7:04	7:06
Oct. 13	5:29	5:54	6:00	6:06	6:14	6:37	6:35	6:19	6:35	5:54	6:03
Oct. 20	5:21	5:39	5:50	5:56	6:04	6:30	6:24	6:08	6:27	5:43	5:54
Oct. 27	5:14	5:25	5:40	5:46	5:55	6:24	6:14	5:57	6:21	5:33	5:47
Nov. 3	4:08	4:12	5:31	5:38	5:47	6:19	6:05	5:47	6:15	5:24	5:40
Nov. 10	4:03	4:00	4:24	4:30	4:40	5:16	4:57	4:39	5:10	4:16	4:34
Nov. 17	3:58	3:50	4:18	4:25	4:34	5:13	4:50	4:32	5:06	4:10	4:30
Nov. 24	3:56	3:42	4:13	4:20	4:30	5:11	4:45	4:27	5:04	4:05	4:27
Dec. 1	3:55	3:37	4:10	4:18	4:28	5:11	4:42	4:23	5:03	4:02	4:25
Dec. 8	3:55	3:33	4:09	4:17	4:27	5:12	4:41	4:22	5:04	4:01	4:25
Dec. 15	3:56	3:33	4:10	4:18	4:29	5:14	4:42	4:23	5:05	4:02	4:27
Dec. 22	3:59	3:35	4:13	4:21	4:31	5:17	4:45	4:25	5:09	4:05	4:30
Dec. 29	4:03	3:40	4:18	4:25	4:36	5:21	4:49	4:30	5:13	4:09	4:34
2024											
Jan. 5	4:08	3:48	4:24	4:31	4:41	5:25	4:55	4:36	5:18	4:15	4:39
Jan. 12	4:14	3:57	4:31	4:38	4:48	5:31	5:03	4:44	5:23	4:22	4:45
Jan. 19	4:20	4:08	4:39	4:46	4:56	5:36	5:11	4:52	5:29	4:31	4:52
Jan. 26	4:27	4:20	4:47	4:54	5:04	5:41	5:20	5:02	5:35	4:39	4:59
Feb. 2	4:33	4:32	4:56	5:02	5:12	5:46	5:29	5:11	5:41	4:48	5:06
Feb. 9	4:40	4:45	5:05	5:11	5:20	5:51	5:38	5:21	5:47	4:57	5:12
Feb. 16	4:46	4:58	5:13	5:19	5:28	5:56	5:47	5:30	5:52	5:06	5:19
Feb. 23	4:51	5:11	5:21	5:27	5:36	6:00	5:56	5:39	5:58	5:15	5:25
Mar. 1	4:57	5:23	5:29	5:35	5:43	6:04	6:04	5:49	6:03	5:23	5:31
Mar. 8	5:02	5:35	5:37	5:42	5:50	6:08	6:13	5:57	6:07	5:31	5:37
Mar. 15	5:07	5:47	6:45	6:50	6:57	7:11	7:21	7:06	7:12	6:39	6:43
Mar. 22	5:12	5:59	6:52	6:57	7:04	7:15	7:29	7:15	7:16	6:47	6:48
Mar. 29	6:16	6:11	7:00	7:04	7:11	7:18	7:37	7:23	7:20	6:55	6:54
Apr. 5	6:21	7:23	7:07	7:11	7:18	7:21	7:45	7:31	7:24	7:03	6:59
Apr. 12	6:26	7:34	7:14	7:18	7:24	7:24	7:53	7:40	7:29	7:10	7:04
Apr. 19	6:31	7:46	7:22	7:25	7:31	7:28	8:00	7:48	7:33	7:18	7:10
Apr. 22	6:33	7:51	7:25	7:28	7:34	7:29	8:04	7:52	7:35	7:21	7:12
Apr. 23		9:07	8:28	8:31	8:36	8:24	9:08	8:58	8:31	8:26	8:10
Apr. 26	6:35	7:58	7:29	7:32	7:38	7:31	8:08	7:57	7:37	7:26	7:15
Apr. 28	6:37	8:01	7:31	7:34	7:40	7:32	8:11	7:59	7:38	7:28	7:17
Apr. 29		9:19	8:35	8:38	8:42	8:27	9:16	9:06	8:35	8:33	8:16
May 3	6:40	8:09	7:36	7:39	7:45	7:35	8:16	8:05	7:42	7:33	7:20
May 10	6:45	8:20	7:44	7:46	7:51	7:39	8:24	8:13	7:46	7:41	7:26
May 17	6:50	8:31	7:50	7:53	7:58	7:42	8:31	8:21	7:51	7:48	7:31
May 24	6:55	8:41	7:57	7:59	8:04	7:46	8:38	8:28	7:55	7:55	7:36
May 31	6:59	8:49	8:02	8:05	8:09	7:49	8:44	8:34	7:59	8:00	7:41

	JERUSALEM	LONDON GMT	N.Y.C. EST	PHILA. EST	WASH., D.C. EST	MIAMI EST	DETROIT EST	TORONTO EST	HOUSTON CST	CHICAGO CST	L.A. PST
June 7	7:03	8:56	8:07	8:09	8:13	7:52	8:49	8:39	8:02	8:05	7:44
June 11	7:04	8:59	8:09	8:11	8:15	7:54	8:51	8:41	8:04	8:07	7:46
June 12		10:32	9:18	9:20	9:23	8:52	10:02	9:55	9:04	9:18	8:49
June 14	7:05	9:01	8:10	8:12	8:17	7:55	8:52	8:43	8:05	8:09	7:47
June 21	7:07	9:03	8:12	8:14	8:19	7:57	8:54	8:45	8:07	8:11	7:49
June 28	7:08	9:03	8:13	8:15	8:19	7:58	8:55	8:45	8:08	8:11	7:50
July 5	7:08	9:00	8:12	8:14	8:18	7:58	8:53	8:43	8:07	8:10	7:49
July 12	7:06	8:55	8:09	8:11	8:16	7:57	8:50	8:40	8:06	8:07	7:47
July 19	7:03	8:48	8:04	8:07	8:11	7:55	8:45	8:35	8:03	8:02	7:44
July 26	6:59	8:39	7:58	8:01	8:06	7:51	8:39	8:28	7:59	7:56	7:40
Aug. 2	6:54	8:28	7:51	7:54	7:59	7:47	8:31	8:20	7:55	7:48	7:34
Aug. 9	6:48	8:15	7:43	7:46	7:51	7:42	8:22	8:11	7:49	7:40	7:27
Aug. 16	6:41	8:02	7:33	7:37	7:42	7:36	8:12	8:00	7:42	7:30	7:19
Aug. 23	6:33	7:47	7:23	7:27	7:33	7:30	8:02	7:49	7:35	7:19	7:11
Aug. 30	6:25	7:32	7:12	7:16	7:22	7:23	7:50	7:37	7:27	7:08	7:02
Sept. 6	6:16	7:16	7:01	7:05	7:11	7:16	7:38	7:25	7:19	6:56	6:53
Sept. 13	6:07	7:00	6:49	6:53	7:00	7:08	7:26	7:12	7:10	6:44	6:43
Sept. 20	5:58	6:44	6:37	6:42	6:49	7:00	7:13	6:59	7:01	6:32	6:33
Sept. 27	5:48	6:28	6:25	6:30	6:38	6:53	7:01	6:46	6:53	6:20	6:23
Oct. 2	5:42	6:16	6:17	6:22	6:30	6:47	6:52	6:37	6:47	6:11	6:16
Oct. 3	6:57	7:22	7:14	7:19	7:26	7:39	7:51	7:36	7:39	7:09	7:11
Oct. 4	5:39	6:12	6:14	6:19	6:27	6:45	6:49	6:34	6:44	6:08	6:14
Oct. 11	5:31	5:56	6:03	6:08	6:16	6:38	6:37	6:21	6:36	5:56	6:05
Oct. 16	5:25	5:46	5:55	6:00	6:09	6:33	6:29	6:13	6:31	5:48	5:58
Oct. 17		6:52	6:53	6:58	7:06	7:25	7:28	7:13	7:24	6:47	6:53
Oct. 18	5:23	5:41	5:52	5:57	6:06	6:31	6:26	6:10	6:28	5:45	5:56
Oct. 23	5:17	5:31	5:45	5:50	5:59	6:27	6:19	6:02	6:24	5:38	5:50
Oct. 24		6:38	6:43	6:48	6:57	7:19	7:18	7:02	7:17	6:37	6:45
Oct. 25	5:15	5:27	5:42	5:48	5:57	6:25	6:16	5:59	6:22	5:35	5:48
Nov. 1	4:09	4:14	5:33	5:39	5:48	6:20	6:06	5:49	6:16	5:26	5:41
Nov. 8	4:03	4:02	4:25	4:32	4:41	5:16	4:58	4:40	5:11	4:17	4:35
Nov. 15	3:59	3:52	4:19	4:25	4:35	5:13	4:51	4:33	5:07	4:11	4:30
Nov. 22	3:56	3:44	4:14	4:21	4:31	5:11	4:46	4:28	5:04	4:06	4:27
Nov. 29	3:55	3:37	4:11	4:18	4:28	5:11	4:43	4:24	5:03	4:02	4:25
Dec. 6	3:55	3:34	4:10	4:17	4:27	5:11	4:41	4:22	5:04	4:01	4:25
Dec. 13	3:56	3:33	4:11	4:18	4:28	5:13	4:42	4:22	5:05	4:02	4:26
Dec. 20	3:59	3:35	4:13	4:20	4:31	5:16	4:44	4:25	5:08	4:04	4:29
Dec. 27	4:03	3:39	4:17	4:24	4:35	5:20	4:48	4:29	5:12	4:08	4:33

HOLIDAYS BEGIN AT SUNDOWN ON THE PRECEDING DAY

	2024	2025	2026	2027	2028	2029	2030	2031	2032	2033	2034	2035	2036	2037
PURIM	Mar. 24	Mar. 14	Mar. 3	Mar. 23	Mar. 12	Mar. 1	Mar. 19	Mar. 9	Feb. 26	Mar. 15	Mar. 5	Mar. 25	Mar. 13	Mar. 1
PESAH	Apr. 23	Apr. 13	Apr. 2	Apr. 22	Apr. 11	Mar. 31	Apr. 18	Apr. 8	Mar. 27	Apr. 14	Apr. 4	Apr. 24	Apr. 12	Mar. 31
LAG BA-OMER	May 26	May 16	May 5	May 25	May 14	May 3	May 21	May 11	Apr. 29	May 17	May 7	May 27	May 15	May 3
SHAVUOT	June 12	June 2	May 22	June 11	May 31	May 20	June 7	May 28	May 16	June 3	May 24	June 13	June 1	May 20
ROSH HA-SHANAH	Oct. 3	Sept. 23	Sept. 12	Oct. 2	Sept. 21	Sept. 10	Sept. 28	Sept. 18	Sept. 6	Sept. 24	Sept. 14	Oct. 4	Sept. 22	Sept. 10
YOM KIPPUR	Oct. 12	Oct. 2	Sept. 21	Oct. 11	Sept. 30	Sept. 19	Oct. 7	Sept. 27	Sept. 15	Oct. 3	Sept. 23	Oct. 13	Oct. 1	Sept. 19
SUKKOT	Oct. 17	Oct. 7	Sept. 26	Oct. 16	Oct. 5	Sept. 24	Oct. 12	Oct. 2	Sept. 20	Oct. 8	Sept. 28	Oct. 18	Oct. 6	Sept. 24
SHEMINI ATZERET	Oct. 24	Oct. 14	Oct. 3	Oct. 23	Oct. 12	Oct. 1	Oct. 19	Oct. 9	Sept. 27	Oct. 15	Oct. 5	Oct. 25	Oct. 13	Oct. 1
SIMHAT TORAH	Oct. 25	Oct. 15	Oct. 4	Oct. 24	Oct. 13	Oct. 2	Oct. 20	Oct. 10	Sept. 28	Oct. 16	Oct. 6	Oct. 26	Oct. 14	Oct. 2
HANUKKAH	Dec. 26	Dec. 15	Dec. 5	Dec. 25	Dec. 13	Dec. 2	Dec. 21	Dec. 10	Nov. 28	Dec. 17	Dec. 7	Dec. 26	Dec. 14	Dec. 3

Published by UNIVERSE PUBLISHING
A Division of Rizzoli International Publications, Inc.
300 Park Avenue South
New York, NY 10010
www.rizzoliusa.com

Design by Tanya Ross-Hughes/Hotfoot Studio
Printed in Hong Kong

Equinox, solstice, and full-moon dates are
given according to Eastern Standard Time
or Eastern Daylight Time as applicable.

2024

January						
S	M	T	W	T	F	S
	1	2	3	4	5	6
7	8	9	10	11	12	13
14	15	16	17	18	19	20
21	22	23	24	25	26	27
28	29	30	31			

February						
S	M	T	W	T	F	S
				1	2	3
4	5	6	7	8	9	10
11	12	13	14	15	16	17
18	19	20	21	22	23	24
25	26	27	28	29		

March						
S	M	T	W	T	F	S
					1	2
3	4	5	6	7	8	9
10	11	12	13	14	15	16
17	18	19	20	21	22	23
24	25	26	27	28	29	30
31						

April						
S	M	T	W	T	F	S
	1	2	3	4	5	6
7	8	9	10	11	12	13
14	15	16	17	18	19	20
21	22	23	24	25	26	27
28	29	30				

May						
S	M	T	W	T	F	S
			1	2	3	4
5	6	7	8	9	10	11
12	13	14	15	16	17	18
19	20	21	22	23	24	25
26	27	28	29	30	31	

June						
S	M	T	W	T	F	S
						1
2	3	4	5	6	7	8
9	10	11	12	13	14	15
16	17	18	19	20	21	22
23	24	25	26	27	28	29
30						

July						
S	M	T	W	T	F	S
	1	2	3	4	5	6
7	8	9	10	11	12	13
14	15	16	17	18	19	20
21	22	23	24	25	26	27
28	29	30	31			

August						
S	M	T	W	T	F	S
				1	2	3
4	5	6	7	8	9	10
11	12	13	14	15	16	17
18	19	20	21	22	23	24
25	26	27	28	29	30	31

September						
S	M	T	W	T	F	S
1	2	3	4	5	6	7
8	9	10	11	12	13	14
15	16	17	18	19	20	21
22	23	24	25	26	27	28
29	30					

October						
S	M	T	W	T	F	S
		1	2	3	4	5
6	7	8	9	10	11	12
13	14	15	16	17	18	19
20	21	22	23	24	25	26
27	28	29	30	31		

November						
S	M	T	W	T	F	S
					1	2
3	4	5	6	7	8	9
10	11	12	13	14	15	16
17	18	19	20	21	22	23
24	25	26	27	28	29	30

December						
S	M	T	W	T	F	S
1	2	3	4	5	6	7
8	9	10	11	12	13	14
15	16	17	18	19	20	21
22	23	24	25	26	27	28
29	30	31				

2025

January						
S	M	T	W	T	F	S
			1	2	3	4
5	6	7	8	9	10	11
12	13	14	15	16	17	18
19	20	21	22	23	24	25
26	27	28	29	30	31	

February						
S	M	T	W	T	F	S
						1
2	3	4	5	6	7	8
9	10	11	12	13	14	15
16	17	18	19	20	21	22
23	24	25	26	27	28	

March						
S	M	T	W	T	F	S
						1
2	3	4	5	6	7	8
9	10	11	12	13	14	15
16	17	18	19	20	21	22
23	24	25	26	27	28	29
30	31					

April						
S	M	T	W	T	F	S
		1	2	3	4	5
6	7	8	9	10	11	12
13	14	15	16	17	18	19
20	21	22	23	24	25	26
27	28	29	30			

May						
S	M	T	W	T	F	S
				1	2	3
4	5	6	7	8	9	10
11	12	13	14	15	16	17
18	19	20	21	22	23	24
25	26	27	28	29	30	31

June						
S	M	T	W	T	F	S
1	2	3	4	5	6	7
8	9	10	11	12	13	14
15	16	17	18	19	20	21
22	23	24	25	26	27	28
29	30					

July						
S	M	T	W	T	F	S
		1	2	3	4	5
6	7	8	9	10	11	12
13	14	15	16	17	18	19
20	21	22	23	24	25	26
27	28	29	30	31		

August						
S	M	T	W	T	F	S
					1	2
3	4	5	6	7	8	9
10	11	12	13	14	15	16
17	18	19	20	21	22	23
24	25	26	27	28	29	30
31						

September						
S	M	T	W	T	F	S
	1	2	3	4	5	6
7	8	9	10	11	12	13
14	15	16	17	18	19	20
21	22	23	24	25	26	27
28	29	30				

October						
S	M	T	W	T	F	S
			1	2	3	4
5	6	7	8	9	10	11
12	13	14	15	16	17	18
19	20	21	22	23	24	25
26	27	28	29	30	31	

November						
S	M	T	W	T	F	S
						1
2	3	4	5	6	7	8
9	10	11	12	13	14	15
16	17	18	19	20	21	22
23	24	25	26	27	28	29
30						

December						
S	M	T	W	T	F	S
	1	2	3	4	5	6
7	8	9	10	11	12	13
14	15	16	17	18	19	20
21	22	23	24	25	26	27
28	29	30	31			